The Free Press Crisis of 1800

LANDMARK LAW CASES

&

AMERICAN SOCIETY

Peter Charles Hoffer

N. E. H. Hull

Series Editors

RECENT TITLES IN THE SERIES:

Murder in Mississippi, Howard Ball

Sexual Harassment and the Law, Augustus B. Cochran III

The DeShaney Case, Lynne Curry

The Battle over School Prayer, Bruce J. Dierenfield

Nazi Saboteurs on Trial, Louis Fisher

Little Rock on Trial: Cooper v. Aaron *and School Desegregation,*
Tony A. Freyer

One Man Out: Curt Flood versus Baseball, Robert M. Goldman

The Treason Trials of Aaron Burr, Peter Charles Hoffer

Griswold v. Connecticut, John W. Johnson

M'Culloch v. Maryland: *Securing a Nation,* Mark R. Killenbeck

The Slaughterhouse Cases, Abridged Edition,
Ronald M. Labbé and Jonathan Lurie

Mapp v. Ohio, Carolyn N. Long

Dred Scott *and the Politics of Slavery,* Earl M. Maltz

The Snail Darter Case, Kenneth M. Murchison

Animal Sacrifice and Religious Freedom, David M. O'Brien

Capital Punishment on Trial: Furman v. Georgia *and the Death Penalty
in Modern America,* David M. Oshinsky

The Michigan Affirmative Action Cases, Barbara A. Perry

The Sodomy Cases: Bowers v. Hardwick *and* Lawrence v. Texas,
David A. J. Richards

The Insular Cases *and the Emergence of American Empire,*
Bartholomew H. Sparrow

San Antonio v. Rodriguez *and the Pursuit of Equal Education,* Paul Sracic

Mendez v. Westminster: *School Desegregation and Mexican-American Rights,*
Philippa Strum

The Confederacy on Trial, Mark A. Weitz

The Times and Trials of Anne Hutchinson, Michael P. Winship

The Miracle Case: Film Censorship and the Supreme Court,
Laura Wittern-Keller and Raymond J. Haberski, Jr.

The Zoning of America: Euclid v. Ambler, Michael Allan Wolf

The Battle for the Black Ballot, Charles L. Zelden

For a complete list of titles in the series go to www.kansaspress.ku.edu.

PETER CHARLES HOFFER

The Free Press Crisis of 1800

Thomas Cooper's Trial for

Seditious Libel

UNIVERSITY PRESS OF KANSAS

Published by the University Press of Kansas (Lawrence, Kansas 66045), which was
organized by the Kansas Board of Regents and is operated and funded by Emporia
State University, Fort Hays State University, Kansas State University, Pittsburg State
University, the University of Kansas, and Wichita State University

Library of Congress Cataloging-in-Publication Data

Hoffer, Peter Charles, 1944–
The free press crisis of 1800 : Thomas Cooper's trial for seditious libel /
Peter Charles Hoffer.
p. cm. — (Landmark law cases & American society)
Includes bibliographical references and index.
ISBN 978-0-7006-1764-7 (cloth : alk. paper)
ISBN 978-0-7006-1765-4 (pbk. : alk. paper)
1. Cooper, Thomas, 1759–1839 — Trials, litigation, etc. 2. Trials (Seditious libel) —
Pennsylvania — Philadelphia. 3. Freedom of the press — United States — History.
I. Title.
KF223.C653H64 2011
345.73'0231 — dc22
2010037922

British Library Cataloguing-in-Publication Data is available.

Printed in the United States of America

10 9 8 7 6 5 4 3 2 1

The paper used in this publication is recycled and contains 30 percent postconsumer
waste. It is acid free and meets the minimum requirements of the American National
Standard for Permanence of Paper for Printed Library Materials Z39.48-1992.

CONTENTS

Preface *vii*

Acknowledgments *xiii*

Prologue: The Pursuit of Benjamin Bache *1*

1. From the Zenger Case to the First Amendment *9*

2. The Federalists Pass a Sedition Act *27*

3. Thomas Jefferson and James Madison Lead a Protest *51*

4. Thomas Cooper's Turn Comes *73*

5. Freedom of the Press on Trial *89*

6. The Unforeseen (and Unintended) Consequences of
   the Sedition Act Crisis *113*

Conclusion: The Paper Barriers *130*

Chronology *135*

Bibliographical Essay *139*

Index *145*

In the first years of the twenty-first century, a terrorist threat from abroad prompted the federal government to consider measures limiting freedom of the press. Congress passed the so-called Patriot Acts, and these included stiff penalties for publishing any information that terrorists might find useful, including, according to Solicitor General Elena Kagan, defenses of the terrorists or their regimes. In a 2010 oral argument defending a prosecution under the acts, she told the U.S. Supreme Court that "the discussion must stop when you go over the line into giving valuable advice, training, support to these organizations." The organizations included those the State Department listed, solely at its own discretion — much like the attorney general's list of subversive organizations in the late 1940s and 1950s. Dissenters called the unitary government's campaign an unprecedented assault on the Bill of Rights and basic freedoms.

The dissenters were wrong. There was a clear precedent for the suppression of freedom of the press: the Sedition Act of 1798. It caused a political furor and it died a sudden death, leaving in its wake bitter political emotions and complex legal questions. The precedent remains.

In the 1790s, seething partisan passions had given rise to standing national political parties, an event that many politicians decried as an invitation to civil disorder at the same time as they aligned themselves with one or the other of the two factions. The Federalists, a party that Alexander Hamilton formed to pass his domestic program, controlled both houses of Congress, the presidency, and the federal courts. They called for a strong federal government aligned with commercial interests and the prompt payment of public and private debts. For the opposition Republican Party, a minority in both houses of Congress, the Federalists were closet monarchists or worse. Republicans preferred a very limited national government and favored the debtor interests.

Party division at home grew even more acerbic when Americans took sides in the wars of the French Revolution. Soon after French reformers called for a constitutional monarchy, the French found themselves at war with Europe's aristocratic states. England, unsympathetic to the radicalism sweeping through France and still bridling at the vital aid the French rendered the American revolutionaries, joined in the conflict against the French. The Federalists sided with the English, even though the Royal Navy was stopping U.S. ships, seizing cargos, and impressing American sailors into service, as well as refusing to honor the peace treaty's provisions for British occupation of forts on the American side of the Great Lakes. A treaty that the Federalists negotiated with England submitted British mercantile claims to arbitration and resolved the border dispute, but did not end the British practice of stopping American ships to look for alleged British sailors. The Federalists saw England's battle against revolutionary France as a war of order and piety against chaos and atheism. To the Federalists, the very existence of the new United States seemed imperiled by foreign agents and their domestic allies. In particular, Federalists regarded immigrants from the British Isles and France whose anti-British sentiments were plain as potential terrorists and feared their league with domestic radicals.

The Republicans denounced the treaty as unpatriotic. To the Republicans, England was a country whose politics and principles were the exact opposite of American republicanism. Revolutionary France, at least in its first years, seemed to represent an experiment in democratic reform inspired in part by the American Revolution. Republicans welcomed expatriate English, Scottish, French, and Irish immigrants into their ranks, created radical "Democratic Republican" societies, and called for more freedom and less government of the Federalist sort.

In the meantime, the French were so incensed at the terms of the treaty the United States had signed with Britain that the French government began to wage an undeclared war against American shipping. The Federalists were delighted with this turn of events and called for a war against France. The Republicans balked at the prospect of a huge army, led by Federalists, gathering at home.

In the midst of this crisis, the Federalist Party majority in Congress passed and President John Adams signed into law four acts that greatly extended the power of the federal government, requiring a loose construction of the Constitution that exceeded anything Alexander Hamilton had proposed in the first years of the new nation and posed a serious threat to the newly ratified Bill of Rights. The Sedition Act was the most far reaching of these four legislative enactments, not only imperiling the freedom to speak in public and write about politics, but setting a precedent for suppression of freedom of speech and the press that lasts to this day. It imposed fines and prison time "if any person shall write, print, utter or publish, or shall cause or procure to be written, printed, uttered or published, or shall knowingly and willingly assist or aid in writing, printing, uttering or publishing any false, scandalous and malicious writing or writings against the government of the United States."

The debate on the Sedition Act and the subsequent trials of opposition-party newspaper editors for attacking John Adams's administration called into question the fundamentals of republican self-government, the relationship between the federal government and the states, and the future of freedom of the press. Did the latter mean no prior censorship, or did the First Amendment imply a more robust liberty? Republican leaders Thomas Jefferson and James Madison prepared resolutions against the acts, which the Kentucky and Virginia state legislatures respectively endorsed. At the center of these resolutions was the doctrine of state "interposition" between the citizens of the states and federal law. Long after the Federalists had passed from the political scene, interposition would come to haunt American politics.

The centerpieces of the Sedition Act crisis were the trials of Republican editors. One of these brought Thomas Cooper into court. A lawyer himself, he was articulate, intelligent, and dedicated to his cause. Unlike others indicted, he was not a scurrilous penman or a paid print assassin. Others who faced trial fled or passed into obscurity, but Cooper would go on to a distinguished career as an educator.

Against him stood one of the most respected and experienced of all the federal prosecutors, William Rawle, and one of the most fearsome Federalists on the bench, Justice Samuel Chase. President John Adams had more than a passing interest, as it was he who ordered Rawle to seek the indictment against Cooper. The trial took place next door to Independence Hall, where Congress was in session. Thus the nation watched as Cooper faced off against the entire Federalist administration.

Although ridden with politics — Cooper turned his defense into an attack on the Federalists — the trial was no mere partisan free-for-all. At stake was the liberty that some Americans thought to be the legacy of the Revolution and others decried as the licentiousness that the Revolution had averted.

Dramatic and portentous at the time, these events had equally striking significance for later American history. The Republicans not only survived the attack, they turned it to their advantage and gained control of the Congress and the presidency in 1801. In that victory, a more capacious view of political dissent seemed to triumph. But no one could have predicted in 1801 that the core notions of the Kentucky and Virginia Resolutions, though framed in the language of the Stamp Act protests, would transform themselves into the doctrine of nullification during the tariff controversies of the late 1820s. Nor was the victory for freedom of the press in 1801 ever complete, for over and over in time of war or near-war, when fears of foreign and domestic terrorism seeped through public discourse, versions of the Sedition Act of 1798 reappeared.

While most modern students of the Sedition Act regard it as an extreme measure motivated as much by partisan malice as by legitimate fears and find the trials unconscionably unfair, a more balanced view takes seriously the arguments on both sides. Surely the legacy of the crisis itself is a vital precedent for anyone concerned about the role of government and the place of dissent in times of national emergency.

The texts that the protagonists in this story created are vital to its significance. They include the defense of editor John Peter Zenger, the fashioning of the First Amendment, the debate in the House of Representatives over the Sedition Act of 1798, the Kentucky and Virginia Resolves, the Thomas Cooper trial record, and John C. Calhoun's "Exposition." These texts as recalled in the pages below constitute an evolving conversation among those who favored greater liberty and those who wanted greater harmony and unity. Both of these qualities are essential in a republican system; it was the relative importance of the two that divided Republicans and Federalists.

The texts themselves have a lasting value to us. They are part of our intellectual, legal, and political heritage. They also speak to modern concerns. For these reasons I have elected to give much space to the actual words spoken and written, quoting copiously. I feel that the authors explained themselves far better than I can paraphrase.

I have tried to give full scope to both Federalists and Republicans in this conversation, but my own views are not hidden. Forced to take sides, as everyone was in the crisis, I would have found myself writing a check for the Thomas Cooper defense fund.

ACKNOWLEDGMENTS

This essay originated as a collection of documents for history and political science students. Sheila Barnett and Brenda Luke at the University of Georgia department of history bravely and diligently transcribed the primary sources of the debates, trial, and newspapers from their electronic and print originals into Word documents. As the manuscript's general introduction and the headnotes to each document grew longer, I concluded that the documents could not simply speak for themselves. When the essay morphed into its present form, I realized that one event stood out from the maelstrom of political controversy. This was the trial of Thomas Cooper. The Landmark Law Cases and American Society series seemed the perfect place for its publication. Or perhaps publication in the series was always in the back of my mind.

I am grateful once again to Mike Briggs, editor and chief at the University Press of Kansas, with whom I have worked for nearly two decades, and to director Fred Woodward and assistant director Susan Schott for countless courtesies. Williamjames Hoffer read the manuscript in an early incarnation, and N. E. H. Hull read it in its near-present form. Both readings were immensely helpful. Earl Maltz, a fellow LLCAS author, kindly read the work with an eye to its suitability for that series. His eye is unfailingly acute. Readers for the press, including Peter Onuf and Douglas Bradburn, were immensely helpful. A very special thank you to Maeva Marcus, whose reading of the manuscript enabled me to correct some real howlers.

The Free Press Crisis of 1800

Prologue

The Pursuit of Benjamin Bache

My story should have been about the trial of Benjamin Franklin Bache for violating the Sedition Act, but death cut that story short. The summer of 1798 was a season of woe in Philadelphia, the new nation's capital. The city sweltered in ninety-degree heat and high humidity. Just as the weather pattern was breaking, young Bache realized that he was dying. That in itself was hardly news in the city. Throughout the 1790s the marshes surrounding the city's wharves bred carriers of malaria and yellow fever. The summer of 1798 had been particularly frightful. The wardens passed by each morning calling, "bring out your dead." The smell of burning clothing taken from the dead lingered over the city like smog.

Bache knew his fate — his aching joints, blood-speckled and putrid vomit, yellowed skin, and high temperature were the telltale signs of deadly yellow fever. Some went mad with the disease, rushing into the streets in their soiled bedclothes. Others lay in immobile torpor, waiting for the end. No one knew what caused the terrible pestilence or what transmitted the disease from victim to victim. Old-fashioned folk remedies did not work, no more than the purging and bleeding the doctors prescribed in their ignorance.

It had happened before — in 1793 — killing nearly one-fourth of the population. Those who could fled the city, including the officers of the federal government temporarily housed in Independence Hall and the surrounding buildings. But the damp, densely packed shops and side streets were full of poor German and Scottish immigrants, slaves and former slaves, refugees from the slave insurrections of the Caribbean, and young people from the surrounding countryside, all too poor to leave. William Penn's "green country town" had become a warehouse of the sick and the despairing.

This was not what the grandson of Benjamin Franklin had planned for himself. Educated partly in Europe, Bache was an erudite, highly literate, and politically passionate journalist. From 1790 to 1798, his *Philadelphia Aurora* had lambasted George Washington, opposed John Adams, and whacked at the Federalists and anything smacking of Anglophilia. On April 20, 1798, for example, he wrote "the impolicy and intemperance of Mr. Adams may yet entail great evils on the United States." Bache paid no courtesies. He wore his passions on his sleeve. Long after others had become doubtful of its violent ways, Bache defended the French Revolution. Willful, daring, impudent, and proud, he knew no fear. The newspaper at its height had a few thousand subscribers; Bache had powerful friends, Jefferson among them, and to his friends Bache was abundant in praise and loyal. But they could not protect him against his enemies, and with each issue of the paper those enemies grew more determined to stop him.

For Bache had pressed the language of republican virtue — the rhetoric of the American Revolution — into the service of partisanship. The virtuous republican was supposed to be above personal interest and party affiliation, sacrificing himself to the good of the people. George Washington was the commonly accepted model of this virtue. But not for Bache. Infuriated by Washington's support for the Jay Treaty with the British, Bache decried the president's aloofness and genteel manner. There was just something about Washington that Bache did not like. Washington was stung by the mosquito bites of the *Aurora*: as he wrote to Jeremiah Wadsworth on March 26, 1797, Bache's "calumnies are to be exceeded only by his impudence, and both stand unrivalled."

Bache was not the only writer who thought Washington had feet of clay. William Duane, another Jeffersonian scribbler, joined in the denunciation of the "father of his country" when Washington stepped down from the highest office. Bache published Duane's diatribe. In turn, Duane helped publish the newspaper on occasion, standing in for Bache. Bache also found a place for a penman more unrelentingly anti-Federalist than Duane — James Thomson Callender, a recently arrived Scottish pamphleteer whom Eric Burns, no mean journalist himself, has described as "a pen for hire, the passionate decade's great journalistic mercenary and perhaps the possessor of its sharpest tongue." It was Callender who had outed Alexander Hamilton's illicit dalliance in 1796, adding to it charges of Hamilton's self-dealing and financial speculation. Though normally a freelance writer, Callender was in 1798 working primarily for Bache and the *Aurora*. A few months later, after his wife died in Philadelphia's yellow fever epidemic, and with his pockets empty, Callender decamped to Virginia. There Jefferson would arrange for Callender to attack Adams, Hamilton, and the rest of the Federalists.

The public prints were full of such fulmination, fueled by a foreign affairs crisis. The French Directory, a conservative inheritor of the French Revolution, was fighting for its life in Europe and had little patience for the U.S. dalliance with Britain. In response to the ratification of the Jay Treaty, the French turned on their former American allies. French privateers stopped British and American ships and confiscated cargo. President Adams tried diplomacy, and, when the French rebuffed it with a demand for a bribe, the Federalists demanded sterner measures. All the while, Bache refused to review or modify his pro-French stance: Were we not grateful to France for its assistance in 1778? Was not our neutrality in France's struggle for survival a violation of basic moral and legal principles? Of course the French were infuriated. They had every right to be. The Federalists had once again pulled the wool over American eyes, Bache wrote.

The response came immediately. Twice a mob attacked Bache's house. Behind the mob was the not-so-unseen hand of the Federalist press, led by John Fenno. His *Gazette of the United States* was to Bache what Bache was to President Adams — unrelentingly spiteful. On May 7, 1798, a Federalist parade turned violent at Bache's door but was driven from the stoop by Bache's friends. Then Fenno's son happened on Bache (who had called the young man "the dirty tool of a dirty faction") in the street, and a fracas followed. Bache replied to Fenno's punches with a whack on the head with a cane. A week later, a Federalist named Abel Humphreys assaulted Bache without warning in a shipyard. The war of words had turned violent.

But Bache did not turn away. For two cents one could purchase his twelve-page pamphlet, *The Truth Will Out! The Foul Charges of the Tories against the Editor of the Aurora Repelled by Positive Proof and Plain Truth and His Base Calumnators Put to Shame.* (Perhaps he had not read his grandfather Benjamin Franklin's famous anecdote on how to shorten titles.) In it, Bache took on "the tools of the British faction" who had been "basely libeling him" on the floor of Congress and in the newspapers. In particular, Fenno's paper, a "pensioned" government mouthpiece, could not be trusted by any right-thinking American, "even the most credulous." For the "hatchers of conspiracy" in Congress had more than Bache as their target. They meant to destroy American liberties just as surely as their British friends had during the Revolution. Unlike Callender, who made his money—or tried to—as a freelance, and unlike Federalist scribblers such as William Cobbett and Fenno, Bache actually believed in a democratic egalitarianism. He resented well-born privilege and aristocratic posturing. He was proud of his grandfather Benjamin, but not for lineage or inheritance. Franklin's irony punctured the hauteur of the rich and powerful. Bache aspired to do the same.

John Adams, no great respecter of the rich or the powerful himself, nevertheless was sick and tired of being Bache's target. Even Abigail Adams weighed in, writing to Mary Cranch on May 10, 1798, that Bache was "wicked and base" and that his criticism of her husband would lead to a "civil war." Though Adams was not a subscriber to the *Aurora*, apparently his federal attorney general for the district of Pennsylvania, William Rawle, read the paper. It was not an aversion to verbal scurrility that spurred Rawle to demand an investigation of Bache's sources (after all, there was plenty of wanton lying on both sides), but the publication on June 16, 1798, of diplomatic correspondence between the French and Adams before Adams presented it to Congress. "Treason," the Federalists cried, although the investigation proved only that someone in the administration had leaked the documents to Bache. He was not acting as an agent for the French. Bache in fact was a patriot—a patriot whose idea of patriotism did not encompass silent loyalty to those in office. Nothing came of Rawle's investigation.

But Rawle would not give Bache a free pass. More was at stake in the newspaper wars of 1798 than hurt feelings. The nation was young; its economy depended in part on European loans, on trade with European nations and their Western Hemisphere colonies; and Americans could not protect their ships at sea, their coastlines, and their interior lands from foreign depredation. It was a dangerous time for even the boldest editor or writer to attack the Federalists. Add to this the Federalist control of all three branches of the federal government, and Bache's decision to call Adams "blind, bald, crippled, toothless" in the

Aurora, for April 27, 1798, was sheer petulance, even if the old and bald part was true.

On June 26, 1798, Rawle filed an indictment with a federal grand jury against Bache, based on the English common law of "seditious libel." Rawle believed that the federal government could send a private citizen to jail for a false and inflammatory publication tending to weaken public confidence in the government. Bache hired two of Philadelphia's leading lawyers, Alexander James Dallas, at the time secretary of state of Pennsylvania, and Moses Levy, to represent him. He had a strong case. Did not the First Amendment's provision for freedom of the press protect the expression of political opinions? To be sure, it said only that Congress shall make no law "abridging the freedom of speech, or of the press." A prosecution under state seditious libel laws was possible, but Rawle got his indictment from a federal grand jury, and the trial would take place in a federal circuit court.

Libel was both a criminal and a civil (tort) wrong. A libel was a defamatory statement in print that harmed the reputation of the person libeled. (Oral defamation was called slander.) If an individual could show that the defamatory statement was untrue and that it had cost the victim something of value, the victim might sue the defamer and seek monetary damages. A jury would decide whether the defendant had actually written the words, whether they were in fact defamatory, and whether in fact the plaintiff had suffered harm. The extent of the monetary award was left to the jury. Colonial Americans seemed to have had a penchant for calling one another cheats, scoundrels, cuckolds, illegitimate children, and other insults in public and in print. Defamation cases were a staple of colonial courts, but the awards were usually small. The purpose of the whole proceeding was to keep order in the community.

Criminal libel was a defamation punished by public law, and in that case the government was the prosecutor rather than the individual who was allegedly defamed. Penalties were fines and jail time, but these did not go to the person named in the defamatory print. Seditious libel was a libel tending to sedition, an offense punished under English common law and colonial American laws.

In the absence of a federal seditious libel law, could Bache be punished in a federal court under the English law? That is, could the government seek an indictment and bring trial in a federal court for criminal libel based on English precedent? Rawle had convinced the grand jury that the answer to the question was yes.

Dallas and Levy proffered a different answer to that question. They had just represented in federal court Robert Worrall, a craftsman accused of trying to bribe a federal revenue commissioner. The two lawyers argued the indictment was faulty because Worrall had not violated any federal law. Dallas told the presiding judges at the federal circuit court, Samuel Chase of the U.S. Supreme Court sitting with district court judge Richard Peters, that "the judicial authority of the Federal Courts, must be derived, either from the Constitution of the United States, or from the Acts of Congress, made in pursuance of that Constitution. It is, therefore, incumbent upon the Prosecutor to show, that an offer to bribe the Commissioner of the Revenue, is a violation of some Constitutional, or Legislative, prohibition." Chase then asked the prosecutor, Rawle,

> "Do you mean . . . to support this indictment solely at [English] common law? If you do, I have no difficulty upon the subject: The indictment cannot be maintained in this Court." Rawle, answering in the affirmative, Chase . . . delivered an opinion to the following effect. "This is an indictment for an offence highly injurious to morals, and deserving the severest punishment. . . . It is attempted . . . to supply the silence of the Constitution and Statutes of the Union, by resorting to the Common law, for a definition and punishment of the offence which has been committed: But, in my opinion, the United States, as a Federal government, have no common law; and, consequently, no indictment can be maintained in their Courts, for offences merely at the common law. If, indeed, the United States can be supposed for a moment, to have a common law, it must, I presume, be that of England; and, yet, it is impossible to trace when, or how, the system was adopted, or introduced."

The federal government had no power to bring indictments under English criminal law without an enabling statute of Congress.

Worrall ended with a whimper. Peters apparently thought the prosecution well founded; Chase demurred:

The Court being divided in opinion, it became a doubt, whether sentence could be pronounced upon the defendant; and a wish was expressed by the Judges and the Attorney of the District, that the case might be put into such a form, as would admit of obtaining the ultimate decision of the Supreme Court, upon the important principle of the discussion: But the counsel for the prisoner did not think themselves authorized to enter into a compromise of that nature. The Court, after a short consultation, and declaring, that the sentence was mitigated in consideration of the defendant's circumstances, proceeded to adjudge, that the defendant be imprisoned for three months; that he pay a fine of 200 dollars; and that he stand committed, 'till this sentence be complied with, and the costs of prosecution paid.

Within a year, Chase would change his view of the federal common law of crimes. The foremost student of Chase's thinking, Stephen Presser, argues that "it is likely that the other Justices convinced Chase that the existence of subject matter jurisdiction based on a federal common law of crime would be crucial in anticipated prosecutions and legislation for seditious libel. They, and Chase too, probably believed that the federal government needed to punish 'an extremely mendacious press' which, according to the Federalists, fiendishly sought to rip asunder the fabric of federal government" — that is, the Jeffersonian press. The Supreme Court had not spoken on the subject of a federal common law of crimes, and would not until 1812 (when it decided that there was no such federal common law of crimes), but the circuit court in which Bache would be tried had spoken. A statute was needed.

Bache was not alone in facing the wrath of the Adams administration. The administration had filed libel actions in federal court against Republican editor John Daly Burk in New York and planned further action against Duane and Callender. But Bache's planned and much publicized defense strategy had warned Rawle and the other Federalists that Congress must pass an act if the administration was to muzzle the Republican attackers. On the same day that Rawle moved against Bache, the House Federalists did just that — making a seditious libel law part of a four-pronged legislative thrust against the Republicans. The bills included provisions for expelling aliens, extending the waiting period for citizenship to fourteen years from five, and giving to the president the power to name an immigrant an "alien enemy" and summarily expel the individual from the United States. All of these were aimed at the radical English, independence-minded Irish, and revolutionary French immigrant supporters of the Republican Party.

Before the Federalists could make Bache the first victim of the Sedition Act, he fell to a more relentless enemy. He died on September 5, 1798, a few days before his trial was to begin. The yellow fever had cheated the Federalists of their prey. But there were other Republican editors on their list, and soon their attention would focus on Thomas Cooper.

CHAPTER I

From the Zenger Case to the First Amendment

Freedom of the press as we understand it today was not a part of the constitutional legacy that England bequeathed to its American colonies. The term and its accompanying ideal were not even commonly used before 1776. A few daring radicals argued for a freedom of discourse during the English civil wars of the 1640s. John Milton attacked the licensing of prints by the government in *Areopagitica* (1644): "Freedom of writing should not be restrained by a discipline imitated from the Prelates [i.e., Roman Catholic Church censorship of impious and heretical books] and learnt by them from the inquisition." But nothing in his essay precluded prosecution after publication, if the print was libelous or seditious. For Milton, freedom of the press amounted to no prior censorship. The English government and its colonial offshoots did not look kindly on freedom of political prints. Although there were more than a few published criticisms of Parliament and crown ministers of state in the eighteenth century and more still of colonial royal governors, the authors hid behind pseudonyms such as Cato and Common Sense lest they be punished.

To criticize the personnel or the policies of government in print courted prosecution for the offense of seditious libel. False speech about the government, or speech having the tendency to undermine public confidence in the government, was also a felony, the crown prosecutors having the discretion to decide which examples of speech fit either of these overbroad and vague categories. Defendants were entitled to a jury trial, but the only issue of fact that came before the jury at trial was whether the defendant wrote or said the words. According to the leading English jurist of his day, William Blackstone, any publication having "a direct tendency to breed in the people a dislike of their governors" — even if the political opinion was based on substantial truth or was a mere statement of fact—was cause for indictment and trial.

The American colonies "received" the English common law of seditious libel. Open criticism of the home government or its agents in America was subject to prosecution. Still, prosecutions for seditious libel in the regular courts were rare. For example, in 1747, when South Carolina's attorney general sought grand jury indictments of critics of governor John Glen, grand juries declined the invitation to indict. The grand jury reported that an indictment would be "destructive of the liberty of the press, a privilege we enjoy, and has been so justly contended by our ancestors."

The most noteworthy episode of a colonial seditious libel prosecution occurred in New York. In 1734, the crown attorney for the colony of New York prosecuted a printer, John Peter Zenger, for seditious libel of New York's governor William Cosby. The trial concluded with a famous closing argument by Zenger's counsel, Philadelphia lawyer Andrew Hamilton. Hamilton was called in to replace James Alexander and William Smith Sr., Zenger's two New York lawyers, when they were held in contempt of court. The trial, presided over by Cosby's handpicked chief justice James DeLancey, should have been an easy win for the prosecution. Zenger had printed the harsh criticisms of Cosby and defenses of freedom of the press. One of these, on November 19, 1733, included the argument (probably written by Alexander, a political opponent of Cosby's), whose substance Hamilton would champion throughout the trial: "No nation ancient or modern ever lost the liberty of freely speaking, writing, or publishing their sentiments but forthwith lost their liberty in general and became slaves. . . . All the venal supporters of wicked ministers are aware of the great use of the liberty of the press in a limited free monarchy."

The battle over John Peter Zenger's publication of criticisms of Governor William Cosby, in 1733, had grown out of the complex politics of colonial New York. Neither side in the controversy could be proud of its conduct. William Cosby was an avaricious man, and from the moment he arrived in New York, he sought to fatten his wallet. The immediate object of his greed was what he believed to be back salary, currently in the pocket of the acting governor, Rip Van Damm. Van Damm's friends, including powerful members of the former acting governor's council such as Chief Justice Lewis Morris and lawyer James Alexander, resisted, so Cosby created a new Court of Exchequer to hear his own suit. When Morris tried to block this end run around the regular courts, Cosby replaced him on the Supreme Court bench with Morris's longtime enemy James DeLancey. At stake were not only thousands of pounds of Cosby's salary, but the fees and influence that Supreme Court justices had.

Morris upped the ante by anonymously criticizing Cosby in the pages of John Peter Zenger's *New York Weekly Journal*. Zenger, a personal friend of James Alexander, thus became the target of Cosby's ire. When successive grand juries refused to indict Zenger in January and October of 1734, the grand jurors disliking Cosby as much as Morris did, Cosby ordered his attorney general to begin the criminal case with an "information" rather than an indictment. Zenger's New York counsel, James Alexander, objected to this novelty so strongly that Cosby's henchman, Chief Justice DeLancey, held Alexander in contempt and refused to let him continue. The Morris faction had an answer ready: Philadelphia's leading lawyer, Andrew Hamilton.

Hamilton was born in Scotland and immigrated to Pennsylvania, where he practiced law and speculated in land. He was one of the leaders of the Philadelphia bar and served in the colony's legislature. At sixty-three years of age, he had highly reputed skill in arguing cases to the jury that was much admired by other local lawyers, for juries had far more power then than they do now to determine matters of law as well as matters of fact. As well, Cosby's almost universal unpopularity in New York made Hamilton's job of defending Zenger much easier.

The scene of the trial was the city hall, built in 1700 on Wall Street, once the edge of old Dutch New Amsterdam. Three stories, columned in front, stone-sided, with a jail in the basement, the city hall was one of the most imposing buildings in the colonies. It took four years and cadres of slave labor to haul the stones from the old fort at the tip of Manhattan to the city hall site. Inside, the main hall was just as imposing, with elegant woodwork and high windows framing the space. A somewhat redesigned and expanded first floor hall would host the first session of the U.S. Congress in 1789, when New York City was temporary capital of the nation. Pierre L'Enfant, then living in the city and working as a civil engineer, would take charge of the renovations.

Hamilton's argument relied in part on his own reading of English statute law and English common law cases. He assumed that Americans had all the rights that Englishmen claimed. This was an assumption not shared by many in the English government. The king's privy council, including his attorney general and solicitor general, believed that the colonies were ruled under a separate set of laws passed by Parliament that applied only to the colonies. After all, they argued, the colonies were the personal property of the Crown. The colonists had no rights, only privileges that the Crown could take away at its discretion.

Thus Hamilton's defense of Zenger signified more than the exculpation of one printer caught in the web of New York politics. If Hamilton swayed the jury to the printer's side, he would also have made a much larger point. Americans could claim as their own all the rights and privileges of Englishmen. His victory would not set a precedent for later cases (only the rulings of the highest courts set such precedent, and these sat in England), but because it had a second life in print, the very same argument he made could be rehearsed by American revolutionary lawyers as they argued against the absolute supremacy of Parliament during the crisis of 1763–1776. Of course, he could not have known this and might well have blanched at the thought. He was a loyal subject of the king and an admirer of what had become the greatest modern empire. He died in 1741.

Hamilton addressed the jury on August 4, 1735. He did not rely at first on oratorical skill to sway the emotions of the jurors or philosophical flourishes to impress them. Instead, he simply ignored the English law of seditious libel. In England, the truth of published criticism of the government was no bar to conviction — indeed, a true statement or a fact proved might damage the government more than a mere speculation or the expression of a negative view. Instead, Hamilton asked: "How shall it be known whether the words are libelous, that is, true or false, but by admitting us to prove them true, since Mr. Attorney will not undertake to prove them false?" Did not everyone know that Cosby was a greedy and overbearing corruptionist? "Besides, is it not against common sense that a man should be punished in the same degree for a true libel, if any such thing could be, as for a false one? I know it is said that truth makes a libel the more provoking, and therefore the offense is greater, and consequently the judgment should be the heavier." Yes indeed, that was the English law.

Well, suppose it were so, and let us agree for once that truth is a greater sin than falsehood. Yet, as the offenses are not equal, and as the punishment is arbitrary, that is, according as the judges in their discretion shall direct to be inflicted, is it not absolutely necessary that they should know whether the libel is true or false, that they may by that means be able to proportion the punishment?

In short, the seditious libel law placed in the hands of Cosby's hand-picked judges the same arbitrary potential for misuse of official power that had allowed Cosby to nibble away at the public treasury. One can imagine DeLancey, himself a beneficiary of Cosby's illicit largesse, squirming on the bench.

Hamilton knew that Zenger's previous counsel had been held in contempt for implying that the bench was prejudiced against their client, so he couched his own argument in hypothetical form. "For would it not be a sad case if the judges, for want of a due information, should chance to give as severe a judgment against a man for writing or publishing a lie, as for writing or publishing a truth?" It was not a contempt of court to take a swipe at the prosecution, however. "And yet this, with submission, as monstrous and ridiculous as it may seem to be, is the natural consequence of Mr. Attorney's [i.e., the prosecution's] doctrine that truth makes a worse libel than falsehood, and must follow from his not proving our papers to be false, or not suffering us to prove them to be true." If the prosecution (including the obviously biased judges) wanted to be fair, they must let Hamilton explore the possible truth of what Zenger had published. But this was exactly what Cosby did not want to come out of the trial. He wanted to muzzle the Morrisite press, not empower it.

If the judges would not let Hamilton argue against the legality of the charges, Hamilton could propose to the jury that everything Zenger published was fact. This was not actually a defense under the common law, but Hamilton was down to the last card in his hand. Juries at that time in the colonies took upon themselves the dual function of deciding law and rendering verdicts of fact. Actually, in asking them to determine whether the publication was true (rather than whether Zenger was the publisher), Hamilton was asking the jury to do what the bench told him he could not ask of the jury. The law did not admit a defense of the truth of the publication. But nothing stopped Hamilton, now in full cry. "Then, Gentlemen of the Jury, it is to you that we must now appeal for witnesses to the truth of the facts we have offered, and are denied the liberty to prove."

Rubbing salt into the wound, Hamilton made the trial into another occasion to accuse Cosby of misconduct. "The facts which we offer to prove . . . are notoriously known to be true. Therefore in your justice lies our safety. And as we are denied the liberty of giving evidence to prove the truth of what we have published, I will beg leave to lay it down as a standing rule in such cases that the suppressing of evidence ought always to be taken for the strongest evidence; and I hope it will have that weight with you." The Roman jurist and orator Cicero had pioneered this technique at trial — deny that you are doing what you are doing as you are doing it. Hamilton's twist on the law would have made Cicero proud had he been hired for the defense.

Chief Justice DeLancey had heard enough. "No, Mr. Hamilton, the jury may find that Zenger printed and published those papers, and leave it to the Court to judge whether they are libelous. You know this is very common. It is in the nature of a special verdict, where the jury leave the matter of the law to the court." In a special verdict, the jury lets the judge decide if the facts as found by the jury warranted a guilty verdict. Hamilton was ready for this interjection. If the jury could leave the decision to the bench, they could also decide not to leave the decision to the bench. Again, Hamilton did not have the law on his side, but he persisted. "I know, may it please Your Honor, the jury may do so. But I do likewise know that they may do otherwise. I know that they have the right beyond all dispute to determine both the law and the fact. . . . Leaving it to judgment of the court whether the words are libelous or not in effect renders juries useless (to say no worse) in many cases."

Hamilton had prepared the ground for his most audacious and clever trick, turning the law inside out.

Although I own it to be base and unworthy to scandalize any man, yet I think it is even more villainous to scandalize a person of public character. I will go so far into Mr. Attorney's doctrine as to agree that if the faults, mistakes, nay even the vices of such a person be private and personal, and do not affect the peace of the public, or the liberty or property of our neighbor, it is unmanly and unmannerly to expose them either by word or writing.

Hamilton here referred to a civil suit for defamation. Presumably Cosby might have pursued this course.

But when a ruler of a people brings his personal failings, but much more his vices, into his administration, and the people find themselves affected by them either in their liberties or properties, that will alter the case mightily; and all the things that are said in favor of rulers and of dignitaries, and upon the side of power, will not be able to stop people's mouths when they feel themselves oppressed. I mean, in a free government.

Hamilton's thesis was that absent a people's ability to criticize the public conduct of officials, there could be no guarantee of "free government." The logical implication was that the voice of the truth teller was the ultimate guarantor of freedom. To be sure, this argument had some circularity to it—only freedom for the opposition to speak its piece guaranteed freedom for the opposition to speak its piece. But Hamilton's point was broader. For the danger of a government that reserved criticism to itself was the use of its police power to protect misconduct. Note that Hamilton was not making the case for the value of opposition itself, an argument that rested upon a much fuller experience with democratic republicanism in America.

A free press uncovered misconduct. If corruption undermined the entire basis of government something that everyone in eighteenth-century English politics agreed was true—then the press must be left free (a logical conclusion that few in English politics reached). Scandalous publication of the private conduct of officials could be countered by a private lawsuit. But Hamilton argued that the law should not be used to throttle accusations of public malfeasance, especially when they were true. "Our Constitution has—blessed be God—given us an opportunity, if not to have such wrongs redressed, yet by our prudence and resolution we may in a great measure prevent the committing of such wrongs by making a governor sensible that it is in his interest to be just to those under his care."

Hamilton had in very short compass touched all the points that would in time become the basis of the First Amendment. Now it was time to expand the case for Zenger into the case for a general freedom of the press.

And has it not often been seen—I hope it will always be seen that when the representatives of a free people are by just representations or remonstrances made sensible of the sufferings of their fellow subjects, by the abuse of power in the hands of a governor, that they have declared (and loudly too) that they were not obliged by any law to support a governor who goes about to destroy a Province or Colony, or their privileges.

This much was true; when offended by imperial appointment, leading colonists complained loud and long to their contacts in England. They made the lives of the erring officials living hell. Wise governors and other appointees learned to cooperate with colonial elites. Strictly speaking, law did not accord the privilege of defending one's rights against rapacious governors and their hirelings, but

it is a right, which all free men claim, that they are entitled to complain when they are hurt. They have a right publicly to remonstrate against the abuses of power in the strongest terms, to put their neighbors upon their guard against the craft or open violence of men in authority, and to assert with courage the sense they have of the blessings of liberty, the value they put upon it, and their resolution at all hazards to preserve it as one of the greatest blessings heaven can bestow.

Despite instructions to the contrary from Chief Justice DeLancey, Hamilton convinced the jury that truth was a defense against the charge of libeling Cosby. He argued as well that the law and the facts were the jury's to decide. Hoping at best for a victory in public opinion, Hamilton and Zenger were delighted when the jury found Zenger not guilty.

The larger arguments that Hamilton made for freedom of the press were in one sense stillborn, for the Zenger case was isolated as precedent. The outcome of a particular trial in common law courts— whether in the colonies or in the home country—did not change the law. This was particularly true in the colonies, whose courts had the status of municipal tribunals in the grand scheme of imperial rule. Had the high courts in England reached a similar conclusion to that which Hamilton proposed in *Zenger*, the law of seditious libel would have been changed forever. But truth did not become a defense in England until Fox's Libel Act in 1792, and to this day in England the burden of proving that a publication is not libelous lies on the defendant in a libel suit (though there are indications that this plaintiff-friendly legal regime will soon change).

Nor did the verdict in Zenger's case dissuade colonial assemblies when they thought their privilege abused by an editor or pamphleteer. Colonial assemblies' contempt citations of journalists were common. On the eve of the Revolution, there still was no freedom of speech or press in political life. Not that Whig (the name the protestors took for themselves) newspaper editors and editorial writers were silent during the crisis. The closing of the royal courts during the final years of the crisis had the unanticipated consequence of allowing the Whigs to publish their protests in the newspapers, safe from the threat of prosecution. Taking advantage of this unexpected opportunity, future revolutionaries such as Thomas Paine blasted Parliament and Crown in bitter and pointed language. Royal governors were condemned as enemies of the people, veritable traitors, in the very same opinion pieces that extolled freedom of the press. But editors and authors were still careful to sign their writings with pen names or not to identify themselves at all. Seen as a whole, the burst of political dissent in print did not represent an argument for freedom of the press or a proof that the press was free even on the eve of independence. And no freedom was accorded to Loyalist newspapers and editors. They were persecuted by mobs, their presses destroyed and their persons threatened.

The point of this brief history is that when one had the power to suppress one's opponents, freedom of the press was a chimera. No one had the right in law to publish criticism of the government. Lacking a robust theory of freedom of political speech, those who used the phrases "freedom of speech" or "freedom of the press" did so to vindicate their own views, not to defend their opponents' right to the same license.

During the Revolution, opposition to Parliament and the Crown could finally speak under its real name—so long as royal troops were not nearby. But the revolutionary governments were no more friendly to their own opponents' speech than the Crown had been to its critics. Loyalists spoke or published only when they were safely within the lines of the king's army. What the Revolution did to further the cause of freedom of speech and press was almost inadvertent, opening the door to freedom of the press, freedom to petition, and freedom to assemble peaceably to protest grievances rather than exploring the full reach of the doctrine underlying freedom of the press.

For the American Revolution would not have been possible without a highly politicized press, the publication of a wide variety of petitions, and the assemblies of protestors. All of them rested on and expressed the idea of the sovereignty of the people. A vigorous press did not abet disorder, despite what the Loyalists warned. But the revolutionaries were still ambivalent about the doctrine of freedom of the press. The Continental Congress in "To the Inhabitants of Quebec" on October 24, 1774, championed "ready communication of thoughts between subjects [colonists were still "subjects" of the Crown] . . . whereby oppressive officials are shamed or intimidated into more honorable and just modes of conducting affairs." The same Congress then stopped up the mouths of those who criticized the Revolution or the conduct of the new state governments. Almost all of the new states' constitutions made some mention of freedom of the press, but the reference was in hortatory language (freedom of the press was good) rather than precatory language (freedom of the press shall be protected). Only Pennsylvania's first state constitution regarded freedom of speech and writing as a privileged liberty, that "ought not be restrained." At the same time, to ensure conformity of opinion as well as speech, the new revolutionary governments, including Pennsylvania's, imposed loyalty oaths. Not to sign (and then obey) led to expulsion from the state and confiscation of the exile's personal property and real estate. This was not quite hypocrisy (after all, there was a civil war raging and its outcome was anything but assured for the revolutionaries), but such broad and liberal sentiments in favor of freedom of expression hardly comported with such swift and illiberal punishment of dissent.

Most revolutionary theorists regarded the exchange of political opinion as valuable, but none of the states explicitly renounced the old concept of seditious libel. This was not surprising, as most of them explicitly provided for the "reception" of as much of the common law as was previously in force in the colony. As jurist Zephaniah Swift wrote of Connecticut law, in 1795, "we must ascertain the common law to know our own law." The exceptions were any part of the common law that touched the Crown or its claims to ownership of all colonial real estate and some of the more sanguinary portions of the English criminal law. Still, the great English law commentator William Blackstone was still cited with approval in state courts, and Blackstone's *Commentaries on the Laws of England* condemned as a felony "malicious defamations of any person, and especially a magistrate, made public by either writing, printing, signs or pictures, in order to provoke him to wraith, or expose him to public hatred, contempt, and ridicule." For the "tendency" of such publications was to disturb the public peace. It was "immaterial" in a prosecution for libel of a public figure whether the publication was true or false, for the offense was the likely consequence of the publication, though a private suit for libel could be defended by proving the truth of the charge.

Defending the newly drafted federal Constitution in December 1787, revolutionary lawyer James Wilson explained:

> I presume it was not in the view of the honorable gentleman to say there is no such thing as a libel, or that the writers of such ought not to be punished. The idea of the liberty of the press is not carried so far as this in any country. What is meant by the liberty of the press is, that there should be no antecedent restraint upon it; but that every author is responsible when he attacks the security or welfare of the government, or the safety, character, and property of the individual.

Blackstone was alive and well in the new nation's jurisprudence. Three years later, Wilson, by then an associate justice of the U.S. Supreme Court, told audiences at his lectures on law, "A malicious defamation of any person, published by writing, or printing, or signs, or pictures, and tending to expose him to public hatred, contempt, or ridicule" was punishable by law.

To repeat: if state constitutions had some form of freedom of the press embodied in bills of rights, the very same states continued to prosecute those who defamed public figures. Those in power decried the "scurrility" of their print critics and the "licentiousness" of the opposition press. Even Benjamin Franklin, whose publications could be scathingly critical of government, denounced the political press as "the highest court in America," putting itself above the law and claiming the "privilege of accusing and abusing fellow citizens at their pleasure" or "hiring out their pens and press to others for that purpose." Surely it was an abuse of freedom of speech and press to write libelously of those in power, and those in power should have the discretion to decide when criticism amounted to such an abuse. Revolutionary leaders even quoted Blackstone's views with favor — a posture contrary to their denunciation of English law but two decades previously.

One could go too far in expressing one's discontent with those in power, and the penalties for transgression were fines and jail time. Republican constitutional thinkers accepted truth as a defense in a prosecution for seditious libel, a significant departure from the English precedent. The problem was that not all political opinions were subject to easy tests of truth or falsity. Saying or writing that a governor was bad at his job, biased, or corrupt in his thinking was an opinion plain and simple. It might be expressive rather than probative, showing the author's feelings. Such statements of feeling — particularly those framed in overblown or vituperative language — were still subject to prosecution. Thus the free expression of political ideas stopped at the doorsill of libel of public figures.

It was against such a background that James Madison introduced into Congress a draft of what would become the First Amendment. Madison came from the Virginia gentry. His father was a successful entrepreneur as well as a planter with two thriving plantations. Madison had been in school during the first days of the Revolutionary War at the College of New Jersey (later Princeton) and never served in the Continental army, but he had represented his state at the confederation congress and with Alexander Hamilton had been the moving force behind the calling of a constitutional convention in 1787.

There Madison shined. Madison was not a lawyer, but he was superbly well read in political philosophy, law, history, and related topics. An early and avid believer in the need for a strong central authority, Madison was behind the Virginia Plan to create a national government. He had a hand in framing the bicameral Congress, fashioning separation of powers among the branches of the federal government, and the drafting of the Supremacy Clause, giving to the federal government the final say when states' laws appeared to violate the Constitution. Madison's notes on the debates remain our primary source for the inside story of the constitutional convention. With his allies from New York, Alexander Hamilton and John Jay, Madison authored a series of newspaper essays later called the *Federalist Papers* to aid in ratification of the Constitution in New York.

After his election to the House of Representatives, in 1788, Madison prepared notes on potential amendments to the new Constitution. State ratification conventions sent their recommendations for these, along with their assent to the new government, to the confederation Congress sitting in New York City. On May 4, 1789, in the same building in which Peter Zenger had been acquitted of seditious libel, now remodeled, renamed Federal Hall, and home to the new Congress, Madison rose and announced that in three weeks he would propose amendments to the Constitution. On May 25, the proposal was delayed by other business. Madison used the time to polish his remarks. On June 8, he read to the House of Representatives nine amendments and immediately encountered opposition. It was too soon, some said, while others simply opposed the idea of changing what the federalists (small "f" meaning those who supported the new frame of government) had so arduously framed. Madison turned to a parliamentary device that had served him, and the federalists, so well in the Constitutional convention. He moved that the amendments be sent to a committee, of which he was named a member.

Short, slight of build, conservatively dressed, Madison seemed lost as he moved about L'Enfant's great marble hall. Madison was no orator. He spoke quietly. But his authority derived from his mastery of any subject on which he spoke. Surely throughout the committee sessions and certainly throughout the debates in the House of Representatives, Madison was the driving force behind the amendments, pressing for consideration and ultimately gaining the necessary support in the House. On July 28, that committee reported favorably, and in August the entire House debated the proposal. The Senate debates were not recorded, as the upper house sat "in camera" — behind closed doors. But the Senate began its deliberations on August 25, and, after a conference with a committee from the House to iron out differences, the Senate agreed to the final version of the twelve amendments on September 25.

One important sticking point was Madison's initial plan to place the amendments within the various Articles of the 1787 Constitution. Exhausted, on August 14 he was persuaded to add them at the end. Thus their present form as a Bill of Rights, set off after the original document, a form that has given them special attention, was something of an accident. A second important issue for Madison was a federal prohibition on states' infringing individual rights of press, conscience, and trial by jury. This anticipated the Fourteenth Amendment, but, in the context of slavery, could be read as a protection of slaveholders' rights against state interference. The Senate rejected this proposal, however, and the Ninth Amendment, reserving to the people rights not set out in the previous amendments, was the best that Madison could get.

Madison's studied modesty contained an apology. "The first of these amendments relates to what may be called a bill of rights. I will own that I never considered this provision so essential to the federal constitution, as to make it improper to ratify it, until such an amendment was added; at the same time, I always conceived, such a provision was neither improper nor altogether useless." Honesty, another of Madison's traits, led him to admit why these basic rights were not already in the Constitution. With the federal government in its infancy, he did not wish to offend the federalists with whom he cooperated at the Philadelphia convention. "I am aware that a great number of the most respectable friends to the Government, and champions for republican liberty, have thought such provisions, not only unnecessary, but even improper; nay, I believe some have gone so far as to think it even dangerous."

With even more modesty, though he could hardly have misled members of Congress, he understated the fierce debate of the past year during which anti-federalists inveighed against the absence of a bill of rights in the original Constitution. "I acknowledge the ingenuity of those arguments which were drawn against the constitution, by a comparison with the policy of Great Britain, in establishing a declaration of rights; but there is too great a difference in the case to warrant the comparison." In fact Britain's 1689 "Act Declaring the Rights and Liberties of the Subject and Settling the Succession of the Crown" was an act of the Parliament at the end of the so-called Glorious Revolution. Like the rest of the British Constitution, it was not a foundation of government at all, and could be abandoned at will. "In the declaration of rights which that country has established the truth is, they have gone no farther than to raise a barrier against the power of the Crown; the power of the Legislature is left altogether indefinite." Thus "the great rights, the trial by jury, freedom of the press, or liberty of conscience" were left unprotected in Britain. Thus, "their Magna Charta does not contain any one provision for the security of those rights, respecting which the people of America are most alarmed."

Madison warned that an all-powerful legislature (like England's Parliament) could pose as much danger to republican virtue in the new nation as the untrammeled power of a chief magistrate. "The freedom of the press and rights of conscience, those choicest privileges of the people, are unguarded in the British constitution." As bills of rights in the state constitutions demonstrated, "a different opinion prevails in the United States. The people of many States have thought it necessary to raise barriers against power in all forms and departments of Government and I am inclined to believe . . . they will have a salutary tendency." With the dry tone that characteristically informed his contributions to legislative debate (especially noteworthy here given that the bill of rights he would offer limited what his own legislative body could do), Madison explained, "The great object in view is to limit and qualify the powers of Government, by excepting out of the grant of power those cases in which the Government ought not to act, or to act only in a particular mode."

Now the ticking bomb exploded – for the entire purpose of what would become the First Amendment was to deny Congress's power to diminish the right to speak, worship, assemble, publish, and petition. Madison wanted Congress to pass what amounted to a self-denying ordinance. "In our Government . . . it therefore must be leveled against the legislative, for it is the most powerful, and likely to be abused because it is under the least control." In short, Congress posed the greatest danger to fundamental rights. "It may be thought that all paper barriers against the power of the community are too weak to be worthy of attention . . . yet, as they have a tendency to impress some degree of respect for them, to establish the public opinion in their favor, and rouse the attention of the whole community, it may be one means to control the majority from those acts to which they might be otherwise inclined."

When debate on Madison's proposal resumed, on August 13, 1789, it gained the shape we recognize today. Madison's quiet persistence won adherents. He also accepted changes to his wording. Roger Sherman of Connecticut convinced Madison that the amendments belonged at the end of the document. Perhaps most important, the language "Congress shall pass no law" appeared, but again these words were not in the first instance attached to freedom of expression. Instead, the committee, followed by the majority of the lower house, wanted to prevent Congress from making any law establishing a religion or restricting the free exercise of religion. Freedom of speech and press were covered by the phrase "Congress shall make no law" because they came before the Establishment and Free Exercise portions of the same clause. The Senate rearranged the proposed amendments into twelve, the third of which read "Congress shall make no law abridging the freedom of speech, or of the press." On September 28th, after a series of debates, the House and Senate approved twelve of the amendments and sent them back to the states for ratification. The First Amendment was ratified by nine states within six months, and by two more within two years.

It is significant to note, at least in passing, that Madison did not include and the Congress did not add the language for the amendment proposed at the Virginia ratification convention. The delegates agreed in 1788 that the liberty of the press "cannot be cancelled abridged restrained or modified by any authority of the United States." This far stronger prohibition would have precluded any official federal interference with the freedom to publish political opinions. Had he proposed this language in 1789, and Congress approved it, Madison's 1798 Virginia Resolves against the Sedition Act would have stood on firmer ground.

Nor could Madison foresee — no one could — that loosening the curbs on political speech would enable partisan divisions within the Congress to reach out into the electoral districts and mobilize the first national two-party system. The new extra-constitutional bodies would pit former allies Alexander Hamilton and James Madison against one another, and lead to a test of the First Amendment.

Fiery in his loyalties, brilliant in his conception of the role of government, dapper in his dress, Hamilton had risen from a teenage immigrant to colonial New Jersey from the Virgin Islands without much in the way of prospects — certainly no claim to a first-rank position in the new federal government. Hamilton was not Washington's first choice for secretary of the treasury, but Hamilton had served as Washington's aide during the war, and no one doubted the younger man's abilities or commitment to the new government.

Hamilton insisted that the executive branch take the lead in dealing with the fiscal crisis of the day. He feared that the federal debt could undermine confidence at home and abroad in the new government and brought to Congress in 1790 and 1791 a comprehensive plan for relief of the federal debt and promotion of the economy. He proposed first, to repay the debt at its face value by issuing new bonds ("funding"), and second, to pay the remaining state as well as the federal debt ("assumption"). This would ensure that investors in Europe and businessmen in America would regard the federal government as fiscally responsible. To retire the debt, he asked Congress to pass a tax ("excise") on distilled whiskey, the first of a number of taxes on commodities. In addition, he wanted to charter a Bank of the United States based on the Bank of England model, to provide a safe place for the United States to deposit its income and create an institution to monitor the circulation of "currency" (paper money). Finally, he called for "bounties" (subsidies) to various industries to promote manufacturing. These included higher tariffs and direct payments.

Taken together, Hamilton hoped, these measures would jump-start the national economy, but taken together, his proposals also favored the creditor classes of the Northeast over the farmers of the West and South. Not surprisingly, many in Congress who were creditors agreed with his program. It would mean profits for them and their fellow speculators. Predictably, representatives of debtors objected that Hamilton's ideas would favor a few over the many, in particular the "money power" over the poor. Hamilton's friends became the Federalist Party in Congress, a disciplined and like-thinking majority not to be confused with the loose alliance of men favoring the federal Constitution.

The measures (excepting the bounties) passed, but Madison, who had been only a few years before Hamilton's co-worker in the struggle to ratify the Constitution, was already becoming the leader of a congressional opposition party. Madison and his supporters in Congress believed that Hamilton and his party had to be stopped. They gained a powerful ally in the new secretary of state, Thomas Jefferson, and decided to call themselves Republicans.

In the political ideology that the founders inherited from Britain, political parties were never acceptable. At best they were seen as self-interested cliques, at worst they might be cabals or conspiracies to pull down the government. In Britain, political groups took a much looser form, often amounting to no more than those in power and those out of office. These shifting coalitions sometimes gained the labels of "court" (ins) and "country" (outs), respectively, but the precise meaning of those terms was as shifting as the partisan alliances they represented. In any case, organized opposition to government, even a "loyal opposition," was proscribed by law. Although members of Parliament could object to acts of government during debate, any speech or publication criticizing the government by a private citizen or a member of Parliament out of doors was subject to prosecution as a seditious libel.

The dispute over Hamilton's domestic policies created a two-party system in Congress, and disputes over foreign policy caused both congressional parties to reach out for support from the voters. The center of that foreign policy was the United States' position on the wars that raged between England and France in the 1790s. During and immediately after the French Revolution of 1789, the French had turned to the United States as a model, but, by 1793, French radicals executed the king and queen and declared the country a republic. A "reign of terror" followed, in which certain opponents of the radicals were executed. Much of the rest of Europe, led by Britain, had joined in an alliance against France. The stage was set for the most virulent party conflict the United States had yet seen, driven in part and sustained in the public mind by political commentary in the newspapers.

CHAPTER 2

The Federalists Pass a Sedition Act

The context and the excuse for a federal sedition act was a war scare with France. During wartime, all governments have residual powers to protect the nation. Whether these powers incorporate the suppression of dissent in the name of national unity is a matter for historians and jurists to debate. The verdict of history is clear: suppression of antiwar sentiment is the norm. The verdict of law is less certain, particularly in a legal regime of individual rights protected against government intrusion. The Bill of Rights created such a regime. The Sedition Act crisis was its first test.

The Treaty of 1778 that brought French funding, supplies, troops, and a navy to the aid of the American revolutionaries was a mutual defense pact between the United States and France. Its terms were limited to the duration of the War for Independence, but in honoring those terms the French government nearly bankrupted itself. That fiscal strain in part led to the calling of a National Assembly, and that to the creation of a constitutional monarchy. By 1792, the French political crisis had turned revolutionary, and with radicals leading the way, the monarchy was replaced by a republic. The king and queen were executed early the next year, and a reign of terror descended upon the nation. Asked by the French for support in its war against Britain, President George Washington demurred. He judged that neutrality was the safest course for the new nation.

Madison, Jefferson, and their supporters feared the British and saw the French Revolution, despite its excesses, as an experiment in liberty similar to America's in 1776. But the Federalists favored Britain. They feared the antireligious sentiments of the French radicals and benefited from trade with Britain. By contrast, the Democratic Republican club members wore French tricolored ribbons in their hats, and started calling one another "citizen" after the French revolutionary style of address.

In 1794 these divisions led to the formation of electoral parties, and the opposition Republicans won a slight majority in the House of Representatives. Both parties sponsored newspapers that attacked the other party's leaders and policies. The Republicans accused the Federalists of creating "a privileged order of men" through patronage and Hamilton's financial policies. Even Washington, lauded as the "father of his country," came under criticism from Bache and others. In turn, the Federalists, in the *Gazette of the United States* on October 1, 1798, called the Republicans "democrats, mobocrats, and all other kinds of rats."

Washington's policy of neutrality did not stop the British governor of Canada from telling a council of Indians to destroy American settlements in the Northwest nor prevent the Royal Navy from confiscating more than 150 American ships bound for France. The Republicans seized on these assaults on American sovereignty and honor to urge war against Britain. Seeking to protect American interests and prevent a rupture with Britain, Washington sent U.S. Supreme Court Chief Justice John Jay to Britain to negotiate a treaty. Neither the president nor the chief justice knew that Hamilton was telling the British ambassador everything that was going on in the cabinet and that the British were aware that the Americans were desperate.

The resulting treaty displeased Washington and infuriated the Republicans. The British promised to withdraw their troops from American soil and to open West Indian markets, but said nothing about America's neutral ships on the seas. Worse, the British continued to "impress" (seize) American sailors from U.S. ships and force them to serve on British ships (though in truth some were deserters from the Royal Navy, and others, naturalized American citizens, were still considered subjects of the Crown by English law). The Federalists had a majority in the Senate and ratified the treaty in 1795. In the House, the Republicans threatened to hold up the appropriation (payment) necessary for the treaty, but finally acquiesced. In the streets, however, Republicans paraded effigies of "that damn'ed arch-traitor, Jay."

In 1793, as this diplomatic imbroglio unfolded, an articulate, well-educated English lawyer and businessman debarked at the Port of New York and looked for lodgings. Thomas Cooper was something of a dilettante — not a failure, but disappointed in much that he attempted.

Born to a genteel family in 1759 in the London suburb of Westminster, he spent much of his early life in the industrial midlands of England. Educated at Oxford, he never took a degree. Trained in medicine, he never practiced. He studied law at the exclusive Inner Temple, but there is no evidence that he completed his studies. His family's finances allowed him to invest in textile production, but unlike others of his generation who made their fortunes in the first years of the Industrial Revolution, he went bankrupt.

Cooper's opinions and writings in England were as cross-grained as his career. He opposed the slave trade but did not advocate abolition of slavery. He signed petitions calling for the reform of Parliament but never ran for public office. He advocated freedom of the mind, condemned organized religion, and warned of government intrusion into private affairs. He believed in the value of disinterested inquiry but opined that self-interest was what really motivated human action. He was a reformer in an age when reform ideas were abroad but not yet adopted. In short, Cooper was a man ahead of his time in many ways, but not very comfortable in it.

Cooper's association with supporters of the French Revolution as much as his radical writings brought down on him the very government scrutiny that he decried. Visiting France and reporting back favorably did not help his cause in England, nor did his open admiration for Thomas Paine, nor did the ensuing controversy it brought with conservative politician and essayist Edmund Burke. Cooper narrowly escaped prosecution for "sedition" after attacking the Pitt government's proclamation of May 21, 1792, warning all and sundry against seditious correspondence with foreign powers and scandalous opposition to the government.

A kind of panic was settling on Parliament and the king's ministers of state, a fear that the words of the friends of France would bring riotous consequences in England. When England went to war with France, the die was cast. Defending the French Revolution became a species of treason, and no man who espoused the principles of "liberty, equality, and fraternity" was safe from prosecution. Cooper, who had returned to England to gather up his children and wife, now made clear his decision to emigrate permanently.

Cooper had joined the corps of "radical émigrés" from England and Scotland to the United States. He wrote to a correspondent in

England that America was "a rising country" and England "a falling one." With his wife and five children, he took up residence in Northumberland County, west of Philadelphia, and began the practice of law. His friendship with scientist Joseph Priestley, a fellow émigré, introduced him to members of the American intelligentsia. These men read and admired Thomas Paine's ideas of equality and liberty, including freedom of speech and the press — the works and the man both despised by the Federalists. Before he departed England, Cooper had published an abridgment of Paine's *Rights of Man* for Manchester readers. As Paine had written of the press in 1791, "there ought, therefore, to be in every nation a method of occasionally ascertaining the state of public opinion in which their interest and happiness is included. It is only by neglecting and rejecting them that they become tumultuous." In short, freedom of the press would prevent the very disorders that the Federalists feared would arise from a free and open discussion of government policy.

Cooper watched as the election of 1796 brought the partisanship of the previous six years to a head. For the first time, two candidates contested the presidency and Federalists and Republicans competed for many congressional seats. The language of politics had become brittle as candidates cast aspersions on one another's ideas and personal lives. In his Farewell Address to the nation Washington warned against "factions," a veiled reference to the gains that Republicans were making in their election efforts.

All obstructions to the execution of the laws, all combinations and associations, under whatever plausible character, with the real design to direct, control, counteract, or awe the regular deliberation and action of the constituted authorities, are destructive of this fundamental principle, and of fatal tendency. They serve to organize faction, to give it an artificial and extraordinary force; to put, in the place of the delegated will of the nation the will of a party, often a small but artful and enterprising minority of the community; and, according to the alternate triumphs of different parties, to make the public administration the mirror of the ill-concerted and incongruous projects of faction.

But his admonition went unheard.

At "caucuses" (meetings) of the parties, the Federalists chose Vice President John Adams as their candidate for the presidency. The Republicans named Thomas Jefferson. It was the first genuine national presidential contest. The Constitution provided that the candidate receiving the largest number of electoral votes would be president. The candidate coming in second would be the vice president. Adams won with 73 votes, but some Federalists refused to vote for Adams's running mate, Thomas Pinckney of South Carolina, with the result that Jefferson became vice president. The partisanship that had marked the rise of the parties continued into the election, as Jefferson's friends in Pennsylvania managed to prevent Adams's electors from winning, but in New York, Adams's friends shut out the Jeffersonians. Adams's support came overwhelmingly from the North, Jefferson's from the South.

John Adams had devoted much of his adult life to his state and his country, serving as a diplomat in France, the Netherlands, and Britain. He was a crusty, demanding intellectual, whose deep piety and devotion to the public good vied with his need for fame and his lack of trust in the common people. Even Jefferson, often fed up with Adams's policies and personality, called him "as disinterested [i.e., above partisanship] as the Being that made him." At the time, Adams did not get along well with Jefferson, but Adams did not believe in parties and would alienate the Hamiltonian wing of the Federalists, costing himself reelection in 1800. After Jefferson retired from the presidency, Abigail Adams would persuade the two men to renew the cordial relations that had marked their service to the revolutionary cause.

The nasty language of the campaign spilled over into the first year of Adams's administration. The election had brought to Congress the most partisan of partisans. Men whose first experience of politics had been the Revolution paid no dues to the polite conventions of eighteenth-century genteel politics. Matthew Lyon was typical of the new breed. An Irish immigrant who had fought on the revolutionary side, he hated Britain and the Jay Treaty and all who supported it with a fierce passion. Nothing governed his tongue or his weak anger-management skills. On January 30, 1798, Lyon, incensed at what he thought was the condescending manner of fellow Representative Roger Griswold, insulted Griswold. Griswold replied that Lyon was a coward. Lyon then spat in Griswold's face. On February 15, 1798, the battle resumed, as Griswold entered the Independence Hall chamber where the lower house met and beat a seated Lyon on the head and shoulders with a cane. Lyon roared back defiance and leapt to the fireplace, where he armed himself with a poker. The two men then engaged in a duel with hickory and wrought iron weaponry. The choice of weapons was telling: Griswold, a Federalist from one of the elite families of the Nutmeg State, and Lyon the upstart Vermont brawler, were appropriately armed. No one was hurt, and the House amused itself by debating whether Lyon, the instigator (he spat in Griswold's face) should be censured or expelled.

While Republicans and Federalists (in some cases literally) spat defiance at one another, France's government decided that the Jay Treaty was an insult. The French began seizing American ships and had by 1798 taken more than 300 vessels. Like Washington with the Jay Treaty, Adams did not want war, and he sent a diplomatic mission to France to negotiate a settlement. The French allowed three men (called X, Y, and Z in the correspondence) to solicit a bribe before the French would meet with Adams's delegation. The delegation reported this to Adams, it got out to the Federalist newspapers, and they began to demand war — "millions for defense, but not one cent for tribute" was their slogan. (It would be used many times thereafter in different causes.)

To the Federalists, the threat to national security seemed obvious. All sorts of rumors circulated among Federalists of Republican plots and conspiracies against the federal government. In Philadelphia, the capital, riots erupted between supporters of France and defenders of the administration. Vice President Jefferson reported that prudent men did not leave their houses. Dr. George Logan's attempt at personal diplomacy, including a secret trip to Paris to try to persuade the French to amend their ways, the Federalists construed as a Republican Party effort to subvert the sovereignty of the new nation. Congress passed the Logan Act, still on the books, forbidding such adventures.

Domestic policy differences and party organizations founded on those differences did not really pose a threat to political order. But parties that had fundamentally different ideologies could become so set in their partisanship that the very existence of an opposition party became an invitation to disorder and disloyalty. So the Federalists felt.

The Federalist majority in both houses of Congress, supported somewhat reluctantly by Federalist President John Adams, were gearing up for war against France and passing new taxes to pay for a greatly enlarged army and navy. Officers for the new army were proposed and debated, with Washington to command and Alexander Hamilton to act as second in command. It was a war that the Federalists intended to wage against French irreligion and radicalism. Republicans in and out of office stood in their way.

One way to reduce the chance that the Republicans could undermine the patriotic effort was to deny to French, Irish, and other radically inclined immigrants the right to vote. The Irish voted Republican because of their enmity for England. Not all the French immigrants supported the Republicans, but most did. English political refugees, often radical in their views, would also vote against the Federalists. The Naturalization Act of 1798 lengthened to fourteen years the period of time for these newcomers to gain the rights of citizens. The Alien Enemies Act gave to the president the discretion to deport an immigrant not yet a naturalized citizen when the immigrant's home country was at war with the United States or when such a war was deemed imminent.

> And the President of the United States shall be, and he is hereby authorized, in any event, as aforesaid, by his proclamation thereof, or other public act, to direct the conduct to be observed, on the part of the United States, towards the aliens who shall become liable, as aforesaid; the manner and degree of the restraint to which they shall be subject, and in what cases, and upon what security their residence shall be permitted, and to provide for the removal of those, who, not being permitted to reside within the United States.

It did not define the acts of the alien that might trigger deportation. Thus the alien who faced deportation might have no warning of it, for no particulars of the offending conduct were defined in the statute. An immigrant could not know he was about to be deported until he was denounced. For many of these political émigrés, deportation was a serious matter. The United States was a haven from the punishment they could expect from their home country's authorities. Adams never deported anyone under the terms of the act, but in somewhat modified form, it is still part of the U.S. Code (50 U.S.C. Secs. 21–24).

The Alien Friends Act gave to the president the authority to deport any alien in time of peace without specifying why so long as he judged them dangerous to national security or public order. It also applied to suspected aliens (men who could not document when they became naturalized). The defendant bore the burden of proving that he was native born or already naturalized, a reversal of the burden of proof the prosecution customarily bore. The act terminated in mid-1800. Again, Adams did not use it, but he favored its passage.

The last of the quartet of acts aimed at the Republican opposition was the Sedition Act. Action on the first three was swift. Debate on the Sedition Act consumed an entire month from mid-June to mid-July 1798. Philadelphia in summer is hot and humid, and this summer the congressmen were even hotter. As the Republicans stepped up their attacks on the first three pieces of legislation, the Federalists became even more determined to curb the opposition press with the Sedition Act.

On June 23, James Lloyd of Maryland introduced the sedition legislation in the Senate. The provisions were broad, vague, and sharply worded. Any action or conspiracy to violate federal laws was made a felony. Any publication of "false, scandalous, and malicious" statements that defamed the government, or brought it into contempt or disrepute, or caused anyone to "hate" the government, was subject to fines and imprisonment (a proposed death penalty was later excised from the bill). A practicing lawyer and militia commander who expected to serve in the war against France, Lloyd's views of France and its supporters were dour. A "wrathful spirit" of partisanship himself, he wanted anyone who even whispered support for France to face charges for treason. Hamilton had no qualms about using libel law to hammer his critics. When James Callender had revealed Hamilton's adulterous affair with one Mrs. Reynolds in 1797, Hamilton denounced the opposition's pressmen as using "the most profligate" means "to wear away the reputations which they could not directly subvert." But Hamilton was privately appalled at some of the provisions in the original bill, writing from his New York City law office to his successor in the Treasury, Oliver Wolcott, on June 29, 1798, "I hope sincerely, the thing may not be hurried through. Let us not establish a tyranny."

But most of the Federalists insisted that in the coming war, the country must be united behind the government, which for them was synonymous with the Federalist Party. Federalist newspapers reprinted evidence of universal patriotic support for the proposed act, though in fact many of the letters and petitions that arrived from around the country were planted by Federalist Party supporters. All true Americans, according to the Federalist press, agreed that the Federalists were not a party at all, but the true expression of Americanism and the guarantor of national security, and this "without hesitation or lengthy debates," as one Federalist songster proclaimed. Those who opposed the war effort were not a party either, but a dangerous "combination," a conspiracy against the Constitution. While it was true that many anti-federalists of 1787 had found a home in the Republican Party, and under the old anti-party ideology inherited from England any combination or organization that opposed the governing majority was illicit, saying that Madison was opposed to the Constitution ignored historical facts.

From June 26 to July 10, 1798, the sedition bill was read and debated three times in the House of Representatives, including a long session in the committee of the whole, and themes and variations of the arguments for and against it were rehearsed multiple times. From the first, the Federalists argued that "if there was ever a nation that required a law of this kind, it was this," for the opposition newspapers constituted an "unwarranted and dangerous combination . . . to overturn" the government. Hence the need for both sedition and conspiracy provisions in the bill. With Bache in jail and the likelihood of the Sedition Act passing, Duane wondered "whether there is more safety and liberty to be enjoyed at Constantinople or Philadelphia." The debate flew on in both houses, with editors on both sides running commentary in their newspapers.

Harrison Gray Otis led the charge for the Federalists in the House. Otis went so far as to accuse Edward Livingston of New York, a Republican representative, of "insurrection." Fortunately, Livingston had made his remarks on the floor of the House, protecting him from prosecution for a common law libel in the federal courts. Otis was genuinely convinced that freedom had a natural limit in maliciously slanderous speech. The Massachusetts state constitution said as much. History was also his tutor; indeed, the history of Massachusetts was almost coterminous with his own family's history. If anyone in the state could claim to be an aristocrat (albeit without noble lineage) it was Otis. The nephew of James Otis Jr., one of the first of the Revolutionaries, he was related by marriage or blood to most of the state's Federalist cadre. For his loyalty, Adams would name him federal attorney for Massachusetts, and his constituents would keep him in either federal or state office until his sixties. He then became mayor of his beloved Boston. In later years, he would lead the opposition to Thomas Jefferson's presidency and "Mr. Madison's War" (the War of 1812), even hinting at the Hartford Convention of 1814 that secession was a possibility if the war continued to bankrupt New England. He opposed the admission of Missouri to the Union as a slave state in 1820, and lived long enough to see the seeds of southern secession sown in the Mexican American War of 1846–1848.

Albert Gallatin was the workhorse of the Republican opposition. He had grounds to question the Federalists' innuendo about unpatriotic newcomers. He took personal affront at the hint that he and others like him wanted a French army to set foot on American shores. Born into an elite Swiss family, he emigrated to America in 1780, aged nineteen, in time to serve in the Continental army. He joined the Jeffersonian Party early in the 1790s, but his election as a senator from Pennsylvania was overturned by the Senate in 1793 on a strict party vote. He was then returned to the lower house by his district in the city of Philadelphia. Gallatin's model for freedom of the press was the Pennsylvania state constitution, a far more democratic document than Massachusetts' fundamental law. Pennsylvania was the only state that guaranteed freedom of speech as well as press. After the sedition act crisis, Gallatin served Jefferson and Madison as their secretary of the treasury and was later a diplomat and educator (helping to found New York University). He died one year after Otis, in 1849.

Though both men were at the height of their powers in 1798, one can imagine how tired all the members of the lower house must have been, sitting through the same arguments over and over. It was late in the third session, and all were ready to go home. Still, there were mind-numbing rituals of parliamentary courtesy to follow, on top of which was the routine business of the federal legislative branch. If contemporary accounts of the sessions are accurate, the members did not exactly sit still during all this. In fact, the floor of chamber buzzed with activity, members entering and leaving, carrying on conversations, reading, eating, drinking, smoking, calling out to one another, and otherwise showing less than avid interest in whoever was speaking. That is, unless the speech was offensive to a member; then he would fling his objections directly at the speaker.

None of this deterred Otis and Gallatin from one final, comprehensive rhetorical joust on July 10. It is one of the most intellectually compelling exchanges in the history of American political dialogue. Neither was an orator on the level of a Daniel Webster or a Henry Clay. But the content of what they said limned out perfectly the conservative and liberal agendas for law, government, and republicanism as they stood at the end of the eighteenth century. They offered different views of the relations between the states and the federal government and between the courts and the executive, on the meaning of Article I, Section 8, of the Constitution (allowing to Congress the authority to pass all necessary and proper legislation to fulfill its stated duties), and on whether the Constitution received or incorporated the common law of crimes in England. But the high level of the exchange should not mask its highly partisan underpinnings. Each man thought his opponent's party a menace to the republic.

Otis was a lawyer of great ability, and it is no surprise that his defense of the sedition bill took the form of a legal brief. The keystone of that brief was his interpretation of the Constitution, and, by implication, Otis's assumption that the Federalists of 1798 were the federalists of 1787 defending their achievement. His and their interpretation of the document would then have had the authority of its framers.

The hardest issue for him to handle was whether the Constitution incorporated the English common law. For as James Madison had written to George Washington (both framers of the Constitution) in October 18, 1787, a month after the constitutional convention had finished its work:

What could the Convention have done [about adding the common law to the Constitution]? If they had in general terms declared the Common law to be in force, they would have broken in upon the legal Code of every State in the most material points: they wd. have done more, they would have brought over from G[reat]. B[ritain].

a thousand heterogeneous & antirepublican doctrines, and even the ecclesiastical Hierarchy itself, for that is a part of the Common law.

Could a Federalist majority in Congress do what the framers of the Constitution had explicitly refused to do?

Otis did not ignore the obvious absence of any reference to common law in the Constitution. Instead, he turned that fact on its head. The lack of reference to the common law in the Constitution was proof that the Constitution incorporated the common law.

This construction of the Constitution [the Federalist position] was abundantly supported by the act for establishing the Judicial Courts. That act, in describing certain powers of the District Court, contains this remarkable expression: "saving suitors in all cases the right of a common law remedy where the common law was competent to give it." He could not tell whence this competency was derived, unless from the Constitution; nor did he perceive how this competency applied to civil and not to criminal cases.

In short, Madison was wrong (not hard to argue given politics in 1798), but Chase was also wrong in *Worrall*. (Though Chase was in all probability already rethinking his position on the federal common law of crimes.)

Otis could have argued that the common law question was irrelevant. Nothing in the Constitution forbade Congress from modeling its criminal law on English common law or incorporating common law doctrines in statutes. The states' criminal codes (with the exception of slave crimes) were largely modeled on English common law. Congress had done that innumerable times already with common law criminal and civil procedure, particularly in the Judiciary Act of 1789 and the Process Act of 1789. Had Otis argued along these lines, he would only need to adopt Hamilton's already well-rehearsed views on the elastic quality of the enumerated powers of the Congress.

But Otis was a common-law lawyer, bred to the common law by innumerable hours studying it as a law student and practicing it in court. While the argument that the Constitution incorporated the common law almost too nicely fit his defense of the Sedition Act, this part of his brief was not sophistic. Otis genuinely believed what he was saying; indeed, he believed that incorporation of the common law greatly strengthened the Constitution. Because of incorporation of the common law the Constitution was not just an experiment in republican theory, but rather it rested on five hundred years of tried and tested English legal thinking. Such a foundation for the Constitution reassured Otis and the other Federalists that (under their stewardship to be sure) the new nation would not founder.

The First Amendment seemed to pose another obstacle to the bill. "It was, therefore, most evident to his mind, that the Constitution of the United States, prior to the amendments that have been added to it, secured to the National Government the cognizance of all the crimes enumerated in the bill, and it only remained to be considered whether those amendments divested it of this power." Once again Otis looked to English common law, which he had already found in the Constitution, to overcome the obstacle. "The terms 'freedom of speech and of the press,' he supposed, were a phraseology perfectly familiar in the jurisprudence of every State, and of a certain and technical meaning. It was a mode of expression which we had borrowed from the only country in which it had been tolerated," to wit, England.

But had not the American Revolution barred the way to such borrowing of English ideas? Not so, according to Otis. One strain of revolutionary republicanism, called by later scholars the "civic virtue" ideology, argued that the survival of the republic depended upon the public character of the members of the government. Their disinterested love of liberty, their personal sacrifice to serve in public office, and their high-minded principles ensured the longevity of the great American experiment in independence. Call these qualities into question and the entire moral fabric of republicanism would be rent. Thus the furious scribblings of the opposition party were by their very nature a danger to republicanism. Civic virtue ideology was born and developed in England and came to America from England, and the American Revolutionaries quoted English thinkers as authorities on civic virtue. Whatever accusations the Revolutionaries might level against the Crown and its ministers of state during the revolutionary crisis, the revolutionaries always conceded the Englishness of civic virtue ideology. Thus the Federalists saw no contradiction between their views of republicanism and their debt to English thinkers.

Obviously, the Federalists had never lost their love of England's ways and laws. They saw common law as a bastion of order and a bulwark against French revolutionary chaos and irreligion. They supported the Jay Treaty not because they saw it as fair (Washington himself hesitated for nearly six months, all the while keeping its terms secret, before asking the Senate to ratify it), but because they did not want to go to war against England. Thus they read the First Amendment not only in light of (their own ideas about) the Constitution, but in light of an English common law that had no bill of rights. In short, they interpreted the meaning of the amendment not as a novelty, a new idea, but as an expression of older ideas. Still, Otis's climb was uphill, for the very purpose of the Bill of Rights was to ensure that the new federal government did not do what the British imperial government had done – deny certain basic freedoms to Americans. Otis nevertheless persisted: "This freedom . . . is nothing more than the liberty of writing, publishing and speaking, one's thoughts, under the condition of being answerable to the injured party, whether it be the Government or an individual, for false, malicious, and seditious expressions, whether spoken or written; and the liberty of the press is merely an exemption from all previous restraints."

Again, reducing the "not abridge" language of the First Amendment to "no prior restraint" had only one precedent – English common law. But Otis brushed aside the circular reasoning that underlay the Sedition Act. For he knew that the act would pass and that its armory would be deployed against the Republican press. In a sense, then, his speech was cynical, sounding in technical legal terms but resting on simple political power. He had the votes.

> Mr. Otis concluded by apologizing to the committee for the time he had employed upon topics so familiar to them as the present. He was aware that the right of Congress to legislate upon his subject, appeared to a majority of that House self-evident, and begged to assure them, that he did not mean to insult the understanding of gentlemen by enlarging upon principles so perfectly plain and undeniable. He justified himself only by the occasion.

Why then go on for hours, as he did, as though he held the fate of the bill in his hands and he must convince a skeptical audience? It may have been the habits of a lifetime in legal pleading. In those days, there were no time limits on counsel's presentations, and arguments in court spun out for days and weeks. The most able lawyers were those with the greatest physical stamina, the most imposing oratorical skills, and the will to impose themselves upon the court and the jury for as much time as they could.

He had at hand books of authorities, and freely quoted from them. One can see the books piled up on his desk, a kind of visual aid as he lectured the other representatives.

In support of this doctrine, he quoted Blackstone's Commentaries, under the head of libels, and read an extract to prove that in England, formerly, the press was subject to a licenser; and that this restraint was afterward removed, by which means the freedom of the press was established. He would not, however, dwell upon the law of England, the authority of which it might suit the convenience of gentlemen [i.e., the Republicans] to question; but he would demonstrate that although in several of the State constitutions, the liberty of speech and of the press were guarded by the most express and equivocal language, the Legislatures and Judicial departments of those States had adopted the definitions of the English law, and provided for the punishment of defamatory and seditious libels.

Habit was not the only motive for Otis's leather-lunged performance. Every lawyer took pride in the craftsmanship of his argument. Law was not just a money-making profession. It was an intellectual endeavor. The great lawyers of the day, including John Marshall, Aaron Burr, Patrick Henry, and Otis, vied with one another in learning and elegance of reasoning. Otis performed his speech, aware that some of his rivals for legal practice were no more than an arm's length away. He supposed that his speech would be published as a separate document from the Annals of Congress, adding to his own reputation and promoting the Federalist cause. (It was, twenty years later.)

Like every first-rate lawyer, Otis knew that his would not be the only voice heard. He knew that Gallatin would rise to speak next, and Gallatin had in his favor Pennsylvania precedent. Otis had to confront and show the difference between that precedent and the federal law.

In Pennsylvania they carried matters still further in their Bill of

Rights, we find "that the printing presses shall be free to every person who undertakes to examine the proceedings of the Legislature, or any branch of the Government, and no law shall ever be made to restrain the free right thereof. The free communication of thoughts and opinions is one of the invaluable rights of man, and every citizen may freely write, print or speak, on any subject, being responsible for the abuse of that liberty."

But Otis offered evidence that even in Pennsylvania the law punished sedition. "Yet, in Pennsylvania, a law has been made, and he had heard from the best authority was still in force 'making it high treason to propose a new constitution in that State.'"

Gallatin replied from his seat: "Mr. Gallatin denied the existence of any such law." In parliamentary rules, a speaker has the floor until his time is up, he is called to order by the chair of the assemblage, or he "yields" to another speaker. Gallatin simply spoke from his seat without being recognized by the chair of the session. But his interjection was telling. "Mr. Otis replied that he might, perhaps, have mistaken the precise words, but it was to that effect."

Still, Otis wisely changed the subject.

"If we go to Virginia," said Mr. O., "we shall read in their constitution that the freedom of the press cannot be restrained, except in despotic Governments; but, in the act passed December, 1792 it is provided, 'That if any person shall, by writing or speaking, endeavor to instigate the people to erect or establish any Government, separate or independent of the Government of Virginia, he shall be subject to any punishment not extending to life or member, which the court may adjudge.'"

This was not really on point, for the Virginia statute concerned words that led to criminal acts and regarded treason, not libel. Otis refused to stay on the ropes, however. "They have another act against cursing and swearing, which is merely using the liberty of speech."

Otis's conclusion did not precisely follow from his citations. But he pressed on regardless. "In all these instances, it is clearly understood that to punish licentiousness and sedition is not a restraint or abridgment of the freedom of speech or of the press. He might no doubt multiply these examples, and appeal to the opinions and decisions of many learned Courts and juries; but he would confine himself to the Courts of Pennsylvania." Why Pennsylvania? A sly dig at the reporter of the Pennsylvania cases, the same Alexander James Dallas who was defending Bache. "Mr. O. then read divers extracts from a case found in Dallas's Reports: the *Commonwealth vs. Oswald*, and the opinion of the Chief Justice, which, as he said, avowed and fortified the law with all its distinctions as stated by himself."

Time to sum up:

"Why then," said Mr. O., "are gentlemen so feelingly alive on this subject? Where lies the injury in attempting to check the progress of calumny and falsehood? Or how is society aided by the gross and monstrous outrages upon truth and honor, and public character and private peace that inundate the country? Can there be any necessity of allowing anonymous and irresponsible accusers to drag before the tribunal of public opinion, magistrates, and men in office, upon false and groundless charges?"

The objections to the bill, according to Otis, were purely political. "The [opposition] had made another singular objection to the bill, arising from an apprehension that, by it, a blow was aimed at an individual printer, to whose paper he subscribed, as it was one of the only three or four papers that were open to a free discussion of the measures of the Administration." Surely the opponents of the bill were overly sensitive. "The public approbation and contentment expressed in the daily papers, was the highest and most honorable testimony of the wisdom of public measures" in most of the country's newspapers. Only the Republican press attacked the administration. With this final twist of argument, Otis turned the Republican case back upon itself. Instead of standing for constitutional principle against the Federalists' partisan expediency, the Republicans were the partisans, and the Federalists the defenders of law, order, and the Constitution.

Gallatin now sought and obtained the floor. He too apologized for going over points already discussed. He knew as well that nothing he said would change the outcome of the vote. Why then bother? As with Otis, Gallatin spoke to an audience outside the chamber. If the Republican press could not directly criticize the administration — for that was the chilling effect of the soon to be passed sedition bill—it could reprint the debates in the lower house. He could see editors in the hall taking notes. What he said in opposition to the bill, published in the Republican papers, would effectively do what the Republican editors would not be safe to do when the Sedition Act became law. He could make the Federalist Party appear the agent of a foreign power (England), an engine of oppression, and the very antithesis of the revolutionary spirit. A tall order, but one he relished.

Gallatin was not a lawyer. Nor was he versed in English law or customs. He was, however, brilliant and dogged. He followed Otis's remarks step by step, using the tools of the logician to combat the skills of the lawyer. "Was the bill, in its present shape free from Constitutional objections? Supposing it to be Constitutional, was it expedient? or, to use the words of the Constitution, was it necessary and proper, at present, to pass this law?" The reference to "necessary and proper" raised the possibility that the first article of the Constitution gave, by implication, Congress the authority to incorporate portions of the common law. "The gentleman from Massachusetts (Mr. Otis) had attempted to prove the constitutionality of the bill by asserting, in the first place, that the power to punish libels was originally vested in Congress by the Constitution, and, in the next place, that the amendment to the Constitution, which declares that Congress shall not pass any law abridging the liberty of the press, had not deprived them of the power originally given."

That was not exactly what Otis had said. He had insisted that the common law was already embedded in the Constitution, and that fact allowed the federal government to punish common law libels. Gallatin was not above a little logic chopping to cut Otis down to size. "In order to establish his first position, the gentleman had thought it sufficient to insist that the jurisdiction of the Courts of the United States extended to the punishment of offences at common law, that is to say, of offences not arising under the statutes or laws of the Union—an assertion unfounded in itself, and which, if proven, would not support the point he endeavors to establish."

Gallatin proposed a very different view of constitutional interpretation from Otis's. If a power was not explicitly granted to Congress in the Constitution, Congress could not exercise that power. This was called "strict construction" of the Constitution and was shared by Jefferson and Madison among the Republicans and by everyone who opposed the ratification of the Constitution ten years previously. By contrast, from the first the Federalists, led by Hamilton, had acted under what later scholars have called a "loose construction" of the Constitution, justifying that view under the "necessary and proper" language (a so-called elastic clause) of Article I, section 8. In it, Congress had the authority to do whatever was necessary and proper to effectuate its delegated powers. But "necessary and proper" was itself subject to interpretation. The Republicans read it to mean procedural steps such as setting the length of its daily sessions. The Federalists saw it as allowing a national bank, excise taxes, and bounties to domestic industries – Hamilton's program of 1790–1791, and the Sedition Act.

Gallatin tried to catch Otis in a logical cul-de-sac. For "had that gentleman succeeded in proving the existence of the jurisdiction of the Federal Courts over offences at common law, and more particularly over libels, he would thereby have adduced the strongest argument against the passing of this bill; for, if the jurisdiction did exist, where was the necessity of now giving it?" In short, if Otis's argument were sound, the prosecution of Bache should have gone forward without the Sedition Act. "If the judicial authority of the Federal Courts, by the Constitution, extended to the punishment of libels, it was unnecessary to pass this law." If constitutional, the Sedition Act was redundant. But if it were needed, then it was not constitutional. "The gentleman from Massachusetts himself, by his efforts to obtain this law, had shown that he did not believe that the courts could set in the case of libels, without the assistance of a law; and every gentleman who had spoken in favor of this bill had explicitly declared, as his opinion, that the Federal Courts had no jurisdiction whatever over offences at common law."

One can almost hear the rustling of papers, the murmured objections from the Federalist side of the aisle, and applause and other noises of approval from the Republicans. Gallatin was not going to concede an inch. "The judicial authority of those [federal] courts is, by the Constitution, declared to extend to cases of Admiralty, or affecting public Ministers; to suits between States, citizens of different States, or foreigners, and to cases arising under the Constitution, laws, and treaties, made under the authority of that Constitution." The absence of the common law from the Judiciary Act of 1789 creating the inferior federal courts was as clear and as definitive as the absence of the common law from the Constitution itself. Otis had "confounded two very distinct ideas the principles of the common law, and the jurisdiction over cases arising under it. That those principles were recognized in the cases where the courts had jurisdiction, was not denied; but such a recognition could by no means extend the jurisdiction beyond the specific case defined by the Constitution." Where in the body of the Constitution did it say that Congress had the power to adopt the English criminal law? Nowhere.

Gallatin defended the doctrine of strict construction as an essential part of federalism. "The Government of the Union is not a consolidated one, possessing general power; it was only a federal one, vested with specific powers, defined by the Constitution." To make the limitations of the federal government under the Constitution even clearer, so that even Otis and his party could understand them, "for greater security, it had been provided, by an amendment which now made a part of the Constitution, that the power not delegated to the United States, nor prohibited to the individual States, remained respectively with the States, or with the people." This was the Tenth Amendment, the last of the Bill of Rights. "Hence it was that Congress had no undefined general legislative powers, but that it became necessary for them, whenever they passed a law, to show from what article of that charter under which they acted—from what specific power vested in them by the Constitution—they derived the authority they claimed."

Neither the sedition bill itself nor its advocates had supplied such evidence, according to Gallatin. It would not do to cry that "Congress had the power, generally, to provide for the punishment of any offences against Government." That kind of open-ended grant of power was tyranny, pure and simple, "for any such act might, by [those in power] be called an offence against Government, and made criminal."

On Otis's argument that the First Amendment only barred prior restraint Gallatin heaped scorn. It was "preposterous to say, that to punish a certain act was not an abridgement of the liberty of doing that act . . . it was an insulting evasion of the Constitution for gentlemen to say, 'We claim no power to abridge the liberty of the press; that, you shall enjoy unrestrained. You may write and publish what you please, but if you publish anything against us, we will punish you for it.'" And why now? "Government has existed for more than nine years without the assistance of this law." Gallatin smelled a rat. "This law is not, then, necessary at all times; indeed, it is intended only to last for three years. Let, then, gentlemen prove that that necessity now exists which heretofore did not exist."

Gallatin did not say what everyone in the chamber was thinking. The election of 1800 would be contested by the two parties, and the sedition act allowed the party that controlled all three branches of the federal government to remain in power. "Where is the House to find proofs of that wonderful, yet unknown change in our circumstances? Will they derive their information from the newspaper scraps . . . as if there was anything alarming or novel in paragraphs blaming or attacking certain measures or certain individuals of Government; as if the present Administration felt more afraid of newspaper abuse than former Administrations, or than other men." It was for the Federalists to prove that "it is not their object to frighten and suppress all presses which they consider as contrary to their views; to prevent a free circulation of opinion; to suffer the people at large to hear only partial accounts, and but one side of the question; to delude and deceive them by partial information, and, through those means, to perpetuate themselves in power."

For the Sedition Act's procedural requirements could easily be abused.

In Pennsylvania, if the prosecution was before the State court, the jury would be summoned by the sheriff, but if before the Federal court, the marshal, in that case would summon the jury. The difference in this case was immense; for the sheriff in Pennsylvania was elected by the people, and held his commission for three years, revocable only for misbehavior. The marshal was appointed by the President of the United States, was removable from office at his pleasure, and sometimes held other offices under the Executive.

In short, the marshal was appointed by the very man whom the opposition newspapers targeted. "When the offences were, as under this bill altogether of a political nature; when the supposed crimes to be punished were a libel against the Administration, what security of a fair trial remained to a citizen, when the same men were to be judges and parties?"

Gallatin had raised every objection he could, but when he returned to his seat, all was as it had been previously. The bill passed. On July 14 Adams signed the Sedition Act, along with the Alien Acts, into law. Adams later recalled that he had "recommended no such thing," and he would not use the powers that the Alien Friends and Alien Enemy Acts conferred on him. But he did resent with a passion the criticism that the Republican scribblers had published, and he would press for prosecutions under the Sedition Act.

The threat of prosecution extended beyond the publication of libelous words. Section 1 of the Sedition Act had a provision for conspiracy. Conspiracy is a separate crime, and the elements of the offense are both vague and very encompassing. For example, if an author, editor, or publisher discussed with a second person a plan to publish a libel, the listener would be liable to prosecution under the act. The listener did not have to do anything other than encourage the libeler to face the same punishment. The Federalist editors published the text of the act with glee. The Republican editors read it with anger and fear:

SECTION 1. Be it enacted by the Senate and House of Representatives of the United States of America, in Congress assembled, That if any persons shall unlawfully combine or conspire together, with intent to oppose any measure or measures of the government of the United States, which are or shall be directed by proper authority, or to impede the operation of any law of the United States, or to intimidate or prevent any person holding a place or office in or under the government of the United States, from undertaking, performing or executing his trust or duty, and if any person or persons, with intent as aforesaid, shall counsel, advise or attempt to procure any insurrection, riot, unlawful assembly, or combination, whether such conspiracy, threatening, counsel, advice, or attempt shall have the proposed effect or not, he or they shall be deemed guilty of a high misdemeanor, and on conviction, before any court of the United States having jurisdiction thereof, shall be punished by a fine not exceeding five thousand dollars, and by imprisonment during a term not less than six months nor exceeding five years; and further, at the discretion of the court may be holden to find sureties for his good behaviour in such sum, and for such time, as the said court may direct.

SEC. 2. And be it farther enacted, That if any person shall write, print, utter or publish, or shall cause or procure to be written, printed, uttered or published, or shall knowingly and willingly assist or aid in writing, printing, uttering or publishing any false, scandalous and malicious writing or writings against the government of the United States, or either house of the Congress of the United States, or the President of the United States, with intent to defame the said government, or either house of the said Congress, or the said President, or to bring them, or either of them, into contempt or disrepute; or to excite against them, or either or any of them, the hatred of the good people of the United States, or to stir up sedition within the United States, or to excite any unlawful combinations therein, for opposing or resisting any law of the United States, or any act of the President of the United States, done in pursuance of any such law, or of the powers in him vested by the constitution of the United States, or to resist, oppose, or defeat any such law or act, or to aid, encourage or abet any hostile designs of any foreign nation against the United States, their people or government, then such person, being thereof convicted before any court of the United States having jurisdiction thereof, shall be punished by a fine not exceeding two thousand dollars, and by imprisonment not exceeding two years.

SEC. 3. And be it further enacted and declared, That if any person shall be prosecuted under this act, for the writing or publishing any libel aforesaid, it shall be lawful for the defendant, upon the trial of the cause, to give in evidence in his defence, the truth of the matter contained in Republication charged as a libel. And the jury who shall try the cause, shall have a right to determine the law and the fact, under the direction of the court, as in other cases.

SEC. 4. And be it further enacted, That this act shall continue and be in force until the third day of March, one thousand eight hundred and one, and no longer: Provided, that the expiration of the act shall not prevent or defeat a prosecution and punishment of any offence against the law, during the time it shall be in force.

The Sedition Act was greeted with great acclaim by local Federalist politicians and voters, making Adams a popular political leader for the first time. Later that day, the *Aurora*, with Bache sure to face a new indictment under the Sedition Act, dropped all pretense of moderation. "Ought a Free People to obey the Laws which violate the Constitution they have sworn to support," a mock advertisement for a debate club announced. Congress fled the city and its pestilence, going into recess until the late fall, and Adams departed for the more salubrious air of his home in Braintree, Massachusetts. In Philadelphia, mobs surged through the streets, chanting songs of patriotic ardor and threats to those who opposed war with France. Jefferson hurried home to Monticello, and Madison to Montpelier to plan the opposition to the war, the Sedition Act, and all things Federalist. The new national government poised at the edge of its first true crisis.

CHAPTER 3

Thomas Jefferson and James Madison
Lead a Protest

The final version of the Sedition Act of 1798 omitted the death penalty for convicted libelers and provided for truth as a positive defense to the charges. Its language remained sweeping and general, and indictment under it was still entirely subject to the discretion of federal prosecutors and their grand juries. The vote for the bill had been along strict party lines, demonstrating that the two-party system was now firmly entrenched in Congress and the division between the parties was a matter of ideology, not class, region, or the members' previous stance on the adoption of the federal Constitution.

Should indictments come under the act, a Federalist-appointed marshal would pick a Federalist-leaning jury to hear a case brought by a Federalist prosecutor before a Federalist circuit court bench. While truth was a defense, political opinions were by their nature neither true nor false. They combined fact with a reading of motive and character and a prediction of what would result from the official stance. It was the intemperateness of the language itself (and the prosecution's presumption that such language would lead to overt acts of sedition), rather than the content of the publication, that would be on trial.

The Sedition Act had an expiration date, after the election of 1800. While advocates argued that the act was a wartime measure (expecting that a war with France was near), in fact the precise end date, after March 3, 1801, would ensure that the Federalists could suppress Republican party electioneering and re-entrench themselves in the presidency and Congress before the act expired. Indeed, the act provided "that the expiration of the act shall not prevent or defeat a prosecution and punishment of any offence against the law, during the time it shall be in force."

The Republicans were appalled by the prospect before them. In their minds, the fate of their party and of the Revolution itself hung in the balance. Had the Federalists intended the act only to throw its ominous shadow over the election campaign, that would have been enough to frighten some Republican critics into silence. But no sooner was the act in place than the federal attorneys switched from the common law indictments to indictments under the statute.

In the process of composing their responses in Congress, Republicans had begun to frame a much more robust and tolerant view of political speech than anyone in the colonies or the early states had adopted. For with the Federalists citing patriotism and the dire threat of war with France as reasons for haste, hinting that "criticism of the proposed sedition bill was itself sedition," the Republicans had to find some foundation for continued opposition to the act that went beyond their own dislike of Federalist policies.

While the Republicans conferred among themselves in private , the conspiracy provision sprung its wickedly clever trap. Indictments might be laid against those who read the seditious issues of the opposition newspapers, talked aloud about their concurring opinions, or sent letters to the editors. The response was immediate. Even the staunchest Republicans stopped subscribing to the *Aurora* and other papers, lest they find themselves in federal court charged with conspiracy. The outcome — even if the juries found the editors not guilty (an unlikely prospect) — was that the Republican newspapers would go out of business for lack of readership.

Resistance to the act took courage. Some editors were not deterred by the act, continued to criticize the government, and indeed added the Sedition Act to the list of proofs of Federalist perfidy. Other Republicans, almost all of them lawyers, prepared legal briefs, disquisitions on the meaning of the Constitution, and ultimately a defense of freedom of thought that extended far beyond defense of Republican Party political aims, and found forums in which to promulgate these views that were (relatively) safe from prosecution. In these responses, the Republicans cried that the Federalists had arrogated more power to Congress (and thus to themselves, as they were in the majority in both houses) than the Constitution allowed. The bill was loose construction of that document run amok. The First Amendment had no place for the "no prior censorship" doctrine, for its language "Congress shall make no law" was explicit. Most important, freedom of speech and press let the people decide what to believe, how to vote, and whether an administration or congressional majority deserved the public confidence. The free exchange of political opinion was the surest guarantor of republican liberty.

When the bill became law, the Republicans sponsored public protest meetings. In Kentucky, Virginia, Pennsylvania, and New York these meetings spilled out into the streets. Protestors denounced the Federalists as tyrants. Republican newspapers carried accounts of these impromptu gatherings as if they were the outpouring of general public sentiment, though in fact many of them were organized and staged by local Republican politicians. Still, the signers of the petitions against the acts and the editors who published the petitions ran the risk of prosecution under the very act they decried.

Some leading Republicans found a safe forum for their objections in friendly state legislatures. Statements made by legislators during sessions of their legislatures were privileged, and could not be prosecuted. The foremost examples of these came from the pens of Vice President Thomas Jefferson and Congressman James Madison.

Jefferson was the vice president of the United States when the Senate, over which he presided, debated the Sedition Act. As presiding officer, he did not take part in the debate, and the Senate sat in these years with closed doors, so no record of the speeches made on the bill exists. But if his mouth was stopped, his pen was free, and Jefferson was soon writing long letters to friends and allies, mapping out a strategy to counter the Federalists' campaign.

No one had a better claim to be the penman of the American Revolution than Jefferson. A planter's son, educated at the College of William and Mary and tutored in the law by George Wythe, Jefferson began the practice of law in 1767. He was first elected to the Virginia House of Burgesses two years later. By nature passionate, by intellectual proclivities a voracious reader and free thinker, a believer in the rationality of man and the importance of science, a man of many interests including educational reform, architecture, botany, and astronomy, Jefferson was a true son of the Enlightenment. He was most proud of his sponsorship of a bill to guarantee freedom of worship in Virginia. He himself was a deist, though he did not reveal this fact during his lifetime.

Jefferson was not an articulate public speaker, but his pen was remarkably facile. It found service in the Continental Congress. Jefferson was a strong and early supporter of independence, and took the lead in drafting the Declaration of Independence for the Congress. His opening words, that all men were created equal, and endowed by their creator with inalienable rights to life, liberty, and the pursuit of happiness, have become the watchwords of Americanism.

After his service as the wartime governor of Virginia, Congress named him the new United States ambassador to France in 1785. There he participated in the early stages of the French Revolution. He had doubts about the federal Constitution, particularly the absence of a bill of rights, but after he was recalled to the United States to serve as the first secretary of state, he distinguished himself by his efforts to keep peace on the frontier and to normalize American relations with Great Britain and France, even as they went to war with one another.

Jefferson resigned as secretary of state in 1793, but, before he retired to his Monticello home, he joined with Madison in founding the Republican Party. Elected as vice president in 1796, he presided over the Senate with skill and patience. But privately he became more and more concerned that the Federalist majority was overstepping constitutional bounds. His role in the Sedition Act controversy was central to the opposition. He had watched with mounting alarm from his seat as presiding officer of the Senate during the Sedition Act debates. Years later, he vaguely recalled that Kentucky Republicans John Breckinridge and Wilson Cary Nicholas pressed him to prepare some sort of protest, but more than likely Jefferson himself was the originator of the idea. When he departed Philadelphia in July 1798, he stopped at Madison's home, Montpelier, outside Orange, Virginia, and the two men discussed what must be done. Madison repaid the courtesy in October, by which time Jefferson had already written and passed on his draft resolves. Madison, the junior partner in the collaboration, may or may not have commented on the severity of Jefferson's views. We know that Madison's would be significantly different when he prepared his own draft resolutions for the Virginia legislative session in December 1798.

Jefferson kept his authorship of his resolves secret, a secret not revealed until the end of his life. The resolutions bear all the marks of Jefferson's style of writing. He proposed a form of resistance to federal authority that after his election as president he would explicitly reject. It was well, thus, that he kept his role in the Kentucky Resolutions secret. (Jefferson's authorship was revealed in 1821, in the Richmond *Enquirer*. He never acknowledged it, however.)

The Kentucky Resolves concerned all four of the Federalists' legislative initiatives, not just the Sedition Act. Jefferson saw them as the pieces of a whole, all having the same purpose of suppressing freedom. In response, he borrowed from the Republican congressmen's ideas, adding his own interpretation of the nature of the union, the proper way to interpret the Constitution, and his political philosophy. Although he was never an active anti-federalist, he was not at first happy with the Constitution. Not only did it lack a bill of rights, it appeared to give too much power to a central government. Hence his first resolve: "That the several States composing the United States of America, are not united on the principle of unlimited submission to their General Government; but that, by a compact under the style and title of a Constitution for the United States, and of amendments thereto, they constituted a General Government for special purposes." Later thinkers with different purposes would expand this notion into "states' rights," the theory that the Constitution bound together sovereign states by their own consent, and the federal government could exercise only those powers "delegated" to it explicitly in the Constitution. All other powers were reserved to the states. "Whensoever the General Government assumes undelegated powers, its acts are unauthoritative, void, and of no force." Jefferson added "that the government created by this compact was not made the exclusive or final judge of the extent of the powers delegated to itself."

This bold assertion was at odds with his initial concession of delegated powers, for the Constitution's text included Article VI: "This Constitution, and the Laws of the United States which shall be made in Pursuance thereof; and all Treaties made, or which shall be made, under the Authority of the United States, shall be the supreme Law of the Land; and the Judges in every State shall be bound thereby, any Thing in the Constitution or Laws of any State to the Contrary notwithstanding." In short, when state courts and the federal government disagreed over the proper interpretation of the federal Constitution, the federal government had the final say.

Jefferson's second draft resolution seemed far milder than his first. He argued that nothing in the Constitution permitted Congress to receive the common law of seditious libel. Indeed, the First Amendment instructed Congress to pass no law abridging freedom of the press. But he went on to declare that "all their other acts which assume to create, define, or punish crimes, other than those so enumerated in the Constitution, are altogether void, and of no force." This doctrine, later and in another context, became the basis for the doctrine of "nullification." Under this interpretation of federalism, a state government could announce that a federal law was null and void within that state. It was a potent intellectual weapon in the hands of those who feared federal legislation, but where might it lead if pushed to an extreme?

Before, with the benefit of hindsight, one accuses Jefferson of willfully or negligently laying the groundwork for the Civil War, one should consider that states' rights in 1798 was not quite the same as states' rights in 1860. As Douglas Bradburn has recently argued,

> the states' rights arguments articulated in opposition to the Alien and Sedition Acts, and understood to be a critique of the Federalist national plan of 1798 are better comprehended by their intellectual origins, than from the hindsight of nullification and secession. However later proponents of states' rights might change their concerns, the original proponents of the idea of the sovereign rights of states grounded their arguments in the principles of popular constitutionalism, popular sovereignty, equality, and natural rights embodied in the most revolutionary sentiments of American Independence.

The third resolution stated a literal interpretation of the First Amendment. Jefferson had already taken part in the movement to end the establishment of the Episcopal Church in Virginia, but the means was an act of the state legislature. He thus read the First Amendment not in terms of federal power over the states, but as an echo of the state's "lawful powers respecting" religion, press, speech, and assembly. The states retained "to themselves the right of judging how far the licentiousness of speech and of the press may be abridged without lessening their useful freedom, and how far those abuses which cannot be separated from their use should be tolerated, rather than the use be destroyed." Virginia had a seditious libel law much like the federal law. Indeed, because the Virginia law had no built-in end date, it was far more intrusive than the federal law. But it was Virginia's law, and that satisfied Jefferson. More ironic still, when a New York Federalist editor named Harry Croswell called Jefferson some unpleasant names in 1803, Jefferson approved of New York's prosecution of Croswell. Alexander Hamilton represented the editor and won his freedom. Politics makes strange bedfellows.

The fourth resolution denied Congress the power to legislate for aliens. Although federal citizenship was not constitutionally defined until the Fourteenth Amendment in 1868, Congress had exercised this power from its inception under its power "to establish a uniform rule of naturalization" in Article I, section 8. Jefferson was not technically correct that "alien friends are under the jurisdiction and protection of the laws of the State wherein they are: that no power over them has been delegated to the United States, nor prohibited to the individual States, distinct from their power over citizens."

The fifth resolve concerned the overseas slave trade compromise of 1787, that Congress would make no law respecting the importation of "certain persons" (whom everyone in the convention understood to be slaves) until 1808. Jefferson read the constitutional provision to give to the states the authority to determine all persons who would and would not be permitted to enter and reside in the state. As an issue of law and good policy, immigration has always been a national rather than a state matter. This was true in the British Empire and its colonies. It is true today. Jefferson was engaging in special pleading to protect the Republican voters who had recently arrived in the United States, but the argument was not altogether unreasonable at the time.

The sixth resolution, that the president of the United States did not have the power under the Constitution to order an alien to leave the country, made no sense. The president was the commander in chief and had the power to enter into treaties with foreign powers. These powers were delegated to him and denied to the states explicitly. Incident to these powers must be the authority to expel alien enemies in time of war that the president deemed dangerous to national security.

A seventh resolution rejected the doctrine of loose construction. This was already an article of Republican faith. Jefferson, however, would soon traduce the doctrine himself, when as president he faced emergencies arising from the Napoleonic Wars.

Kentucky's legislature passed the resolves, with modifications (the word "nullification," for example, was excised), and then sent them to the other states. For Jefferson had asked that Kentucky create a "committee of conference and correspondence" to "communicate the preceding resolutions to the legislatures of the several States." Committees of correspondence were the brainchild of Samuel Adams of Massachusetts in 1772 to keep up the momentum of protest against the British Empire. Whether Jefferson meant to duplicate that agitation against the federal government or not, Kentucky did as he asked. No other state subscribed to the Kentucky Resolutions.

The precedent outlived its context and its creator. In 1814, furious that the Jeffersonian Republicans' war with Great Britain was crippling New England's economy, Federalists gathered in Hartford, Connecticut, and resolved:

> That it be and hereby is recommended to the Legislatures of the several States represented in this Convention to adopt all such measures as may be necessary effectually to protect the citizens of said States from the operation and effects of all acts which have been or may be passed by the Congress of the United States, which shall contain provisions, subjecting the militia or other citizens to forcible drafts, conscriptions, or impressments, not authorized by the Constitution of the United States.

When southern states feared that a northern majority in Congress would circumscribe the rights of slaveholders, in 1850, they came together in a convention, recalled the Kentucky Resolves, and repassed them. In 1860, they fulfilled the promise of the resolves, withdrawing from the Union that Jefferson denied was perpetual and indissoluble.

Jefferson, already campaigning for the presidency in 1799, saw the Sedition Act as an issue to be exploited. On January 26, 1799, he wrote what would become his campaign platform to Elbridge Gerry, a fellow Republican. Gerry was a signer of the Declaration of Independence and served in the Confederation government. Although he was a delegate to the constitutional convention in 1787, he originally opposed the federal Constitution as a dangerously anti-republican document, particularly lamenting the absence of a bill of rights. But Gerry did support Washington's administration and was a personal friend of John Adams.

Gerry became a Jeffersonian Republican in reaction to the Sedition Act. Later, as governor of Massachusetts, Gerry continued to oppose the Federalists. He was the originator of the "Gerrymander," a reapportionment plan that would have created a single salamander-like electoral district out of the Federalist-dominated coastal portions of eastern Massachusetts, thereby limiting Federalist electoral strength in the state legislature and the federal Congress. He would serve as James Madison's second vice president. A maverick in his political affiliation, Gerry was also an independent thinker.

When Thomas Jefferson explained his political philosophy to Gerry, he valued Gerry as a fellow revolutionary theorist as well as a political ally. He claimed to be a friend of the federal government — true enough, as he had served it faithfully as secretary of state and vice president. "I do then, with sincere zeal, wish an inviolable preservation of our present federal constitution, according to the true sense in which it was adopted by the States." But he was opposed to "monarchising its features by the forms of its administration, with a view to conciliate a first transition to a President & Senate for life, & from that to a hereditary tenure of these offices, & thus to worm out the elective principle."

Jefferson pledged his allegiance to the First Amendment's call for religious liberty ("Congress shall make no law respecting an establishment of religion or prohibiting the free exercise thereof"). Jefferson was privately a deist, publicly a Christian, and devoutly an enemy of superstition. "I am for freedom of religion, & against all maneuvers to bring about a legal ascendancy of one sect over another: for freedom of the press, & against all violations of the constitution to silence by force & not by reason the complaints or criticisms, just or unjust, of our citizens against the conduct of their agents." Recent events had annealed his idealism. "I was a sincere well-wisher to the success of the French revolution, and still wish it may end in the establishment of a free & well-ordered republic; but I have not been insensible under the atrocious depredations they have committed on our commerce." No doubt again thinking of the possible publication of the letter, or at least of Gerry's circulating it among friends, Jefferson concluded:

The first object of my heart is my own country. In that is embarked my family, my fortune, & my own existence. I have not one farthing of interest, nor one fiber of attachment out of it, nor a single motive of preference of any one nation to another, but in proportion as they are more or less friendly to us. . . . These, my friend, are my principles; they are unquestionably the principles of the great body of our fellow citizens, and I know there is not one of them which is not yours also.

In the darkest hour of the Republican Party, Jefferson saw a ray of light. "The unquestionable republicanism of the American mind will break through the mist under which it has been clouded, and will oblige its agents to reform the principles & practices of their administration."

While Jefferson was planning his campaign, Virginia Republicans were calling for some kind of protest against the Sedition Act. Madison agreed to draft resolves to place before the state assembly when it met in December 1798. Madison knew the general outlines of Jefferson's argument, but whether he saw a draft before he prepared his own is uncertain. He presented his work to a committee of the Virginia House of Delegates. The draft was debated on December 21, 1798. It passed three days later.

Madison's part in the Republican opposition had always been more open than Jefferson's. Early in 1790, Madison became disenchanted with Hamilton's economic program for the new federal government, and, from his seat in the House of Representatives, Madison organized opposition to Hamilton's proposals. Madison played the major role in the creation of the Republican Party, toured the northeast with Jefferson in 1792 to drum up support for the party, and later led the floor fight against the Jay Treaty. Madison would go on to serve as President Thomas Jefferson's secretary of state, then for two terms as president of the United States, and finally would retire as a revered elder statesman. He died in 1836.

Unlike Jefferson, Madison believed in a strong central government. Thus his resolves were different from Jefferson's in significant ways. But like Jefferson, Madison did not take public credit for the draft. He gave it to Wilson Cary Nicholas, who examined it and prepared a defense of it, should one be needed, then transmitted the draft to John Taylor of Caroline, a Republican state legislator, to introduce it at the next session of the assembly.

Having served exclusively in the legislative branch (while Jefferson's experience was as a governor of Virginia and a diplomat), Madison recognized the need to state general principles and leave administrative decisions to others. Just about everyone then and later recognized that the Virginia Resolves were far more moderate than the Kentucky Resolves.

Madison began, "Resolved, that the General Assembly of Virginia, doth unequivocally express a firm resolution to maintain and defend the Constitution of the United States, and the Constitution of this State, against every aggression either foreign or domestic, and that they will support the government of the United States in all measures warranted by the former." To make the point even stronger, he continued, "That this assembly most solemnly declares a warm attachment to the Union of the States, to maintain which it pledges all its powers; and that for this end, it is their duty to watch over and oppose every infraction of those principles which constitute the only basis of that Union, because a faithful observance of them, can alone secure its existence and the public happiness." Whether he meant to emphasize the word "Union" or the phrase "of the States" was the sticking point. The preamble to the Constitution did not refer to a union of the states. It began "we the people" and continued "in order to form a more perfect union." Madison did not write these words. But they were there nonetheless. On its face, the Constitution was not a league or association or compact among entirely sovereign states over which the federal government had no authority.

Madison used the term "compact," but did not press for an overarching compact or contract theory of the union. Instead, he elected to embed the notion of compact in a discussion of delegated powers, thereby limiting the former idea. "That this Assembly doth explicitly and peremptorily declare, that it views the powers of the federal government, as resulting from the compact, to which the states are parties; as limited by the plain sense and intention of the instrument constituting the compact; as no further valid than they are authorized by the grants enumerated in that compact." But this was not enough to counter the Federalists' program, and Madison dipped his toe into dark waters. "In case of a deliberate, palpable, and dangerous exercise of other powers, not granted by the said compact, the states who are parties thereto, have the right, and are in duty bound, to interpose for arresting the progress of the evil."

Interposition was not quite the same as nullification, but it did traduce a central and absolutely necessary tenet of federalism. Both the federal and the state governments were sovereign. That meant the federal government had authority over persons residing in the United States. Nullification struck down federal law. Interposition allowed the state to prevent the law from affecting people in the state. In effect, interposition denied the sovereignty of the national government.

Madison did not explore the implications of the term or the concept behind it, and the rest of the resolves were admonitory, a kind of "tsk, tsking" at how mean-spirited and dangerous the Federalists were. "That the General Assembly doth also express its deep regret, that a spirit has in sundry instances, been manifested by the federal government, to enlarge its powers by forced constructions of the constitutional charter which defines them." Madison saw a plot behind the Alien and Sedition Acts "to consolidate the states by degrees, into one sovereignty, the obvious tendency and inevitable consequence of which would be, to transform the present republican system of the United States, into an absolute, or at best a mixed monarchy." The reference to monarchy was a staple Republican charge. Nothing in the acts themselves spoke of monarchy. Indeed, Adams had been, by some accounts, reluctant to sign the acts and hesitant to deploy them. It was the legislative branch — Congressional Federalist majorities — that had pushed for the acts. Adams hated the monarchy, in particular the English Crown.

Madison finally got down to brass tacks. "The General Assembly doth particularly protest against the palpable and alarming infractions of the Constitution, in the two late cases of the 'Alien and Sedition Acts' passed at the last session of Congress . . . which acts, exercises in like manner, a power not delegated by the constitution, but on the contrary, expressly and positively forbidden by one of the amendments thereto." Madison now sounded the general alarm, the argument against government curbs on a free press that remains the most potent: the Sedition Act gave to those in office "a power, which more than any other, ought to produce universal alarm, because it is leveled against that right of freely examining public characters and measures, and of free communication among the people thereon, which has ever been justly deemed, the only effectual guardian of every other right."

Here Madison was on firm ground, his "guardian of every other right" brilliantly adapting a phrase first used to defend the right to private property.

Madison could speak with authority about the meaning of the First Amendment, having written it and sponsored it in Congress. He recalled that he had based his draft on Virginia's constitutional provision for freedom of the press. "The Liberty of Conscience and of the Press cannot be cancelled, abridged, restrained, or modified by any authority of the United States" because of the amendment. "It would mark a reproachable inconsistency, and criminal degeneracy, if an indifference were now shown, to the most palpable violation of one of the Rights, thus declared and secured."

There was a final provision, much like Jefferson's, that called the Alien and Sedition Acts "unconstitutional, and not law, but utterly null, void, and of no force or effect." Who wrote or added this provision remains unclear. Perhaps it was someone on the committee, perhaps even Jefferson, who was on hand for the debate. But Henry Lee urged that the assembly drop this language, and wise heads prevailed. It did not appear in the printed version, at least.

In a step less provocative than Jefferson's, Madison asked Virginia to "solemnly appeal to the like dispositions of the other states, in confidence that they will concur with this commonwealth." No revolutionary committees of correspondence were necessary. If other states' legislatures joined their general sentiments with Virginia's, the obnoxious acts would surely be repealed. Though the election of 1800 was still a year away, Madison had his eye on the races for Congress. Candidates from states such as Virginia, declaring themselves in opposition to the Alien and Sedition Acts, would take notice of local feeling.

During the debate, Federalist George Taylor pleaded with his fellow delegates to drop the phrase depicting the federal Constitution as a "compact, to which the states alone are parties" from the body of the resolves. The implication of the phrase was that the federal government was simply a contractual agreement among the states. Madison did not believe this to be so, and had argued against it in his contributions to the *Federalist* papers. The language of his draft was much closer to Jefferson's views in 1787 than to Madison's at that time. Taylor convinced the Republican majority to omit the single word "alone," a halfway compromise. The lower house adopted the draft, voting 100 to 63. On December 24, 1798, Virginia transmitted the resolves to the other states.

The Federalists in the assembly were not mollified by the amendments. A minority report by the Federalists, signed by fifty-eight delegates, was also circulated. Federalist newspapers in Virginia and elsewhere decried the resolves as forewarning a civil war. The stage was set for the coming elections.

Madison soon had second thoughts. Had he said too much? Too soon? In too forceful a way? Had he traduced his own understanding of the sovereignty of the federal government resting upon the people of the United States rather than the states alone? Unlike Jefferson, who felt little concern about the inconsistencies in his ideas, Madison liked to keep to the straight and narrow path. Thus while Jefferson was writing to Gerry, Madison was composing learned mini-treatises. On January 7, 1800, the Virginia assembly issued a report, drafted by Madison, on freedom of expression. It brought together many of the arguments that Republicans had made against the Sedition Act and placed them in the larger contexts of constitutional history and the American Revolution. It is a remarkable piece, worthy of the author of some of the most persuasive (and in future years most quoted) of the *Federalist* newspaper essays Madison, Hamilton, and John Jay wrote in 1787 and 1788 to aid ratification of the federal Constitution in New York.

In fact, Madison used the 1800 report as an occasion to address Hamilton. Although his former ally was nowhere mentioned in the report, Madison periodically mentioned the intentions of the framers of the Constitution, hinting that Hamilton should return to the sentiments he had expressed in 1788. In the *Federalist* pieces the three framers had authored, all took great pains to explain how limited the powers of the new federal government would be. Madison was thus reminding Hamilton how he, flushed with power, had overstepped the boundaries set in 1788. It was to prevent just such misconduct that amendments were necessary.

Perhaps most important, Madison's argument for freedom of the press had unintended logical implications. Madison was not a democrat in the modern sense of the word. When he wrote about "the people" he did not mean individuals, he meant the people as a whole, represented by the better men. He did not believe in extending the right to vote or full participation in the political process to women, racial minorities, and the poor. For him and most of his colleagues, democracy was dangerous, for it empowered the mob. But if one follows the logic of his argument, it leads in the direction of greater participatory democracy. The actual consequence of arguments like this in the next twenty years was more democracy. Property qualifications for voting and holding office vanished from state constitutions. Political parties reached out to "the common man" for support. A democratic revolution swept over the country.

First, Madison covered old ground. Though he was not a lawyer, his analysis of the constitutional issues would have done Otis or Hamilton proud.

> Whenever, therefore, a question arises concerning the constitutionality of a particular power, the first question is, whether the power be expressed in the Constitution. If it be, the question is decided. If it be not expressed the next inquiry must be, whether it is properly an incident to an express power, and necessary to its execution. If it be, it may be exercised by Congress. If it be not, Congress cannot exercise it.

Seditious libel was not mentioned in the Constitution. Could Congress pass such a law within the scope of the elastic clause? No. For it was not necessary and proper for the operation of Congress. The law protected the president, not Congress. Nor was a seditious libel law necessary to prevent insurrections. Mere words could not cause the American people to rise up against their government, unless that government was so wicked that revolution was warranted. No one pretended that this situation existed.

In fact, the Federalists did claim that such a danger was at hand. They feared the influence of the French. They feared the radicalism of the Republicans. And most of all they feared that if war came, criticism of the government would weaken its ability to prosecute the war. From his home at Mount Vernon, Washington repeatedly wrote to Adams that strong measures must be taken to keep the nation safe from internal as well as external enemies. The "arts" of deception of the French, "and those of their agents [in America] to countenance and invigorate opposition" required strong countermeasures.

Madison did not know about Washington's letters to Adams (in any case the father of his country had passed away the previous year), but Madison had heard the Federalists in Congress and read Fenno and the other Federalist publicists. Adams's own views were known as well. Madison chided all of them: "But it surely cannot, with the least plausibility, be said, that the regulation of the press, and a punishment of libels, are exercises of a power to suppress insurrections." The Federalists were either hysterical themselves or cynical fearmongers.

Again and again, Madison cited his authority as a framer of the Constitution. He was modest but firm. "It must be recollected by many, and could be shown to the satisfaction of all, that the construction here put on the terms 'necessary and proper' is precisely the construction which prevailed during the discussions and ratifications of the Constitution." He was there. He kept notes. The very fact that some elastic clause was deemed necessary was a proof that it "cannot too often be repeated, that . . . the peculiar character of the Government, is possessed of particular and definite powers only, not of the general and indefinite powers vested in ordinary Governments." Had the federal government possessed indefinitely extendable powers, there would have been no need for "necessary and proper" language. He thus turned the Federalist argument for basing the Sedition Act on the necessary-and-proper clause of the Constitution on its head. The clause proved the limited character of the national government, not its infinite extension.

Madison wrote the First Amendment. He should know what it meant. Today this mode of interpreting the meaning of the Constitution is called "original intent." In original intent, the modern interpreter ascertains the meaning that the framers assigned to constitutional language and applies it to the issue at hand. Original intent faces the obstacle that modern interpreters cannot know precisely what the framers were thinking. But ten years later, Madison certainly knew what he had been thinking in 1789. (Though whether or not his own thinking can be equated with the meaning of the words that became the First Amendment is an issue that constitutional scholars and theorists continue to debate.) "The next point which the resolution requires to be proved is that the power over the press exercised by the Sedition Act is positively forbidden by one of the amendments to the Constitution."

The amendment spoke in these words: "Congress shall make no law respecting an establishment of religion, or prohibiting the free exercise thereof, or abridging the freedom of speech or of the press; or the right of the people peaceably to assemble and to petition the Government for a redress of grievances." The Federalists (whom Madison neglected to mention were also at the Philadelphia constitutional convention) tried to "vindicate the Sedition Act" by contending "that the 'freedom of the press' is to be determined by the meaning of these terms in the common law." But the federal Constitution mentioned nothing about Congress having the authority to adopt the common law — a point Madison had already hammered home.

Madison correctly recalled that the Federalists proposed that "the article [i.e., the First Amendment] supposes the power over the press to be in Congress, and prohibits them only from abridging the freedom allowed to it by the common law." But in this, as in so much else, the Federalists missed the essential difference between English common law and American law. "In the United States the case is altogether different. The People, not Government, possess the absolute sovereignty. The Legislature, no less than the Executive, is under limitations of power." There was no residual authority in the federal government to do whatever a majority in it wanted to do. "In the United States the great and essential rights of the people are secured, against legislative as well as against executive ambition. They are secured, not by laws paramount to prerogative, but by constitutions paramount to laws." The entire purpose of a Constitution, the be-all-and-end-all of America's revolutionary achievement, was to limit government infringement of individual rights.

Madison next clarified his conception of checks and balances. One of his major contributions to the debates at the constitutional convention was his discussion of the system of checks and balances. (Though, ironically, it was John Adams's 1776 *Thoughts on Government* that made the earliest strong case for separation of powers.) In the *Federalist* essay Number 51, Madison had explained:

To what expedient, then, shall we finally resort, for maintaining in practice the necessary partition of power among the several departments, as laid down in the Constitution? The only answer that can be given is, that as all these exterior provisions are found to be inadequate, the defect must be supplied, by so contriving the interior structure of the government as that its several constituent parts may, by their mutual relations, be the means of keeping each other in their proper places.

For example, the president had the veto power, but Congress could override the veto. The president nominated the judges, but the Senate had to confirm them. The president could enter into treaties, but the Senate had to ratify them.

Adjunct to these direct checks and balances was the notion that any of the three branches might overreach itself. This was certainly true when it came to suppressing dissent. As he continued in the *Federalist*, "it is of great importance in a republic not only to guard the society against the oppression of its rulers, but to guard one part of the society against the injustice of the other part. Different interests necessarily exist in different classes of citizens. If a majority be united by a common interest, the rights of the minority will be insecure." Freedom of the press was one such right.

He expanded on these views in 1800: "This security of the freedom of the press requires that it should be exempt not only from previous restraint by the Executive, as in Great Britain, but from legislative restraint also; and this exemption, to be effectual, must be an exemption not only from the previous inspection of licensers, but from the subsequent penalty of laws." He was consistent when he reminded the Virginia legislators that "in the United States the executive magistrates are not held to be infallible, nor the Legislatures to be omnipotent; and both being elective, are both responsible."

Was he aware at this point that the very same reasoning applied to the Virginia legislature? Madison was not only learned, he was astute. Although he directed his comments to the Federalists in Congress, he was also lecturing his Virginia neighbors. Jefferson had relied upon a robust notion of state sovereignty, the forerunner of states' rights theory. Madison intentionally avoided that line, resting his case upon a concept of republicanism. Defense of freedom of the press flowed far more naturally from his thinking than from Jefferson's. Jefferson was apparently content with state prosecutions of editors for seditious libel. Madison was not.

It was because of this variation from Jefferson's resolves that Madison mischaracterized the state practice. "In every state, probably, in the Union, the press has exerted a freedom in canvassing the merits and measures of public men of every description which has not been confined to the strict limits of the common law." That simply was not true; Virginia prosecuted editors for libels of public figures. So did other states. But Madison needed to contrast state with federal law in order to protect writers such as Callender, whose refuge was not far from where Madison sat. "And it will not be a breach either of truth or of candour to say, that no persons or presses are in the habit of more unrestrained animadversions on the proceedings and functionaries of the State governments than the persons and presses most zealous in vindicating the act of Congress for punishing similar animadversions on the Government of the United States."

Knowing that his facts were wrong, Madison hedged: "Whatever weight may be allowed to these considerations, the committee [of the Virginia legislature] do not, however, by any means intend to rest the question on them. They contend that the article of amendment, instead of supposing in Congress a power that might be exercised over the press, provided its freedom was not abridged, was meant as a positive denial to Congress of any power whatever on the subject." Otis had gotten his facts wrong too. That did not excuse Madison. Indeed, it was his command of fact that gave his presentations, whether in Congress or not, such authority. Why did he get his facts wrong here? He certainly knew better.

At least his narrative of the origin of the bill of rights was factually correct. "To demonstrate that this was the true object of the article, it will be sufficient to recall the circumstances which led to it, and to refer to the explanation accompanying the article. When the Constitution was under the discussions which preceded its ratification, it is well known that great apprehensions were expressed by many . . . of the freedom of the press particularly." The absence of a federal bill of rights might expose these rights "to the danger of being drawn, by construction, within some of the powers vested in Congress."

During the debates in the Virginia ratification convention in 1788, "it was invariably urged" (by Madison among others) "to be a fundamental and characteristic principle of the Constitution, that all powers not given by it were reserved; that no powers were given beyond those enumerated in the Constitution." This was not sufficient to allay suspicions and concerns about the willingness of a majority in Congress to exceed their powers. Ruefully Madison conceded that the anti-federalists at that time had a point. "It is painful to remark how much the arguments now employed in behalf of the Sedition Act are at variance with the reasoning which then justified the Constitution, and invited its ratification."

In Virginia and "in so many of the [ratification] Conventions," the debate had focused on "whether the doubts and dangers ascribed to the Constitution should be removed by any amendments previous to the ratification, or be postponed in confidence that, as far as they might be proper, they would be introduced in the form provided by the Constitution. The latter course was adopted." But the promise behind it, a promise that Madison himself made to voters when he first ran for his seat in the House of Representatives, was that amendments would be offered as soon as the new government assembled. "Among those rights, the freedom of the press, in most instances, is particularly and emphatically mentioned." Madison was far more assertive than he had been when he introduced the amendments ten years earlier. Then, prudence counseled a modest tone. Now, provocation counseled a "firm and very pointed manner."

Time to finish:

> Is then the Federal Government, it will be asked, destitute of every authority for restraining the licentiousness of the press, and for shielding itself against the libelous attacks which may be made on those who administer it? The Constitution alone can answer this question. If no such power be expressly delegated, and if it be not both necessary and proper to carry into execution an express power — above all, if it be expressly forbidden, by a declaratory amendment to the Constitution — the answer must be, that the Federal Government is destitute of all such authority.

That is, it could not throw sticks and stones back at those who only threw words at its officers. "The unconstitutional power exercised over the press by the Sedition Act ought, more than any other, to produce universal alarm; because it is leveled against that right of freely examining public characters and measures, and of free communication among the people thereon, which has ever been justly deemed the only effectual guardian of every other right."

Was Madison inventing a new concept of freedom of expression? He and Jefferson were Enlightenment thinkers. That is, many of their ideas of freedom of expression were rooted in earlier eighteenth-century notions. Such notions had led French *philosophes* such as Voltaire and Diderot to claim a freedom for the mind that even enlightened monarchs found objectionable. But did such grand claims for freedom of thought extend to the legal protection of free expression of thought? The notion of no prior censorship that the Federalists attached to the First Amendment did not contradict the ideal of free expression on its face. One could say, as Adams and others did, that freedom of expression was fine, but licentious and seditious speech and publication was punishable. Leonard Levy believes that Madison and Jefferson had come up with something new. Madison and Jefferson would have denied that they had innovated. Instead, they claimed a sound revolutionary rights base for freedom of the press. The First Amendment simply committed the federal government to protect what some states already protected. They argued that the power to punish political opinion undermined freedom of the press so profoundly as to reduce it to nullity.

Madison was still haunted by his flirtation with interposition, and many years later, when Virginia's legislature veered toward adoption of a full-blown doctrine of nullification, Madison spoke out against it privately. On the one hand, he wished devoutly that the political concussions of the day would subside. He had never been comfortable with an excess of party passion. On the other hand, he worried that his own words could become, indeed were becoming, the basis for a doctrine of disunion.

If Madison's measured words that winter of 1799–1800, far more than Jefferson's angry fulminations, became part of the lexicon of First Amendment interpretation, that was little comfort for the two Virginians. The election of 1800 was still far off, and the Federalists were tuning up the machinery of suppression. The Sedition Act prosecutions ground slowly but surely. The federal attorneys were already busy hounding the Republican press. Indeed, they had picked a perfect target.

With Bache gone, Lyon seemed a natural to become the first victim of the Sedition Act. In 1798, Lyon started his own newspaper in Vermont to attack the Federalists, titled, appropriately, *The Scourge of Aristocracy and the Repository of Important Political Truths*. Lyon had not lost his appetite for brawling, and Federalists loved to caricature him as "the beast" and "Mat the Democrat" (when democrat meant mob leader). Lyon did have a nasty tongue, which prudence never tamed, and his efforts to "oppose truth to falsehood, and to lay before the public such facts as may tend to elucidate the real situation of the country" ran to the lambasting of "every aristocratic hireling . . . down to the dirty hedge-hogs and groveling animals" of the Federalist press and party, as he wrote on October 1, 1798. The axe fell swiftly. Between October 6 and October 9, 1798, he was indicted, tried, and found guilty of malicious defamation in Rutland, Vermont. The speed of the entire proceeding (the jury returned a guilty verdict on the same day that the trial began) was a tribute to the machinery assembled to prosecute these cases. Jailed, he was reelected to Congress by his constituents. When the Federalists again attempted to retry him after his release, in February 1799, this time for his jailhouse publications (pen and paper were surreptitiously given him), he decamped from Vermont. When in 1802 he reappeared in Kentucky, he was again elected to Congress. He died in Arkansas, in 1822, a man who preferred a wild country to one filled with Federalists.

CHAPTER 4

Thomas Cooper's Turn Comes

As the year 1800 opened, political rhetoric reached fever pitch. As far as Federalists were concerned, Republican political writers were "Jacobins, Democrats, and enemies to God and Man . . . journeymen [printers] of discontent and sedition." Republicans replied in kind. James Duane's *Aurora* of March 18 hissed, "What can the public think of a party whose impotent vengeance is directed against such men as Jefferson . . . and who deign to employ such wretched tools for their calumny as Fenno?"

Ideological differences fueled the flames, but a more practical and less disinterested motive for the caterwauling on both sides was the coming election. Originally, the two parties were gatherings of men in office—parties within the government. By 1800, they had become electoral parties with local organizations dedicated to placing their party's men in power. The newspaper war was a struggle for public opinion. If prosecutions (or the threat of prosecution) under the Sedition Act were effective, the Republican press would be crushed. The Federalists would then find it far easier to retain control of the presidency and Congress. In this scenario, the prosecution of Republican editors promised vital short-term partisan gains. And conviction was likely with Federalist judges presiding over trials before Federalist jurors picked by federal marshals (though no one proved that the marshals weeded out Republicans).

Leading the charge from inside the Adams administration against the Republican publicists was a hard-line conservative Federalist lawyer from Salem, Massachusetts, Secretary of State Timothy Pickering. Harvard educated, Pickering entered the law profession before the Revolution, and during the War for Independence served as Washington's adjutant general and then as quartermaster general. Whether these posts whetted his appetite for speculation or he simply joined other elite lawyers such as Aaron Burr, Alexander Hamilton, and James Wilson in the rush to get rich after the war, Pickering found himself embroiled in a series of real-estate schemes. Washington bailed him out by making him postmaster general (a lucrative patronage position). Pickering later served as U.S. Indian commissioner (another way to keep an eye out for prospective land grabs) and became secretary of state under Adams. In this post he lobbied hard for a war with France. A bitter man, he had a bitter view of the Republicans.

No one could mistake his frame of mind. For example, on September 29, 1798, Pickering wrote and arranged for the publication of his response to a critical letter from the electors of Prince Edward County, Maryland, directed to President Adams. In it, Pickering explained why the Sedition Act was necessary. "The sedition act . . . prescribes a punishment only for those pests of society, and disturbers of order and tranquility . . . who stir up sedition, or abet the hostile designs of any foreign nation." No law should permit the uttering of "false and malicious" opinions. Indeed, the very objections that the Prince Edward voters expressed were a slur upon the good name of Congress (that is, the Federalist members of Congress), who had "so tender and regardful" a concern for the rights of Americans that they made truth a defense and provided for jury trial.

Pickering was not content for the prosecution of such dangerous men to take its natural course. He began to set snares for unwary Republican writers, and no one fit this bill better than Thomas Cooper. In 1799, Pickering wrote and arranged for Fenno to publish an attack on Cooper calling him a hypocrite. By 1799, Cooper was regularly critical of the Adams administration, but, two years before, with a family of five children to feed, he had applied to Adams for a judicial appointment in western Pennsylvania. Pickering's anonymous slur was a clever trap, and Cooper fell into it.

After reading the anonymous denunciation, Cooper went ballistic. He wrote and published a broadside entitled "To The Printer" on November 2, 1799, which he signed, that accused "the president himself" of spreading "falsehoods." Though Cooper still thought well of Adams's "intentions," his "underlings" were capable of "anything." His target in this was Pickering, whose authorship of the anonymous piece Cooper might or might not have recognized. It did not matter. Cooper's reply was barbed: "Is this the letter of a man, or not? I do not appeal to the cowardly propagator of anonymous falsehoods, but to the public."

Thus far, there was nothing in the broadside that fit the definition of seditious libel. But Cooper did not stop with a defense of his own honor. The broadside contended that in 1797, when Cooper had sought federal office, "Mr. Adams had [not yet] . . . interfered as president of the United States to influence the decision of a court of justice—a stretch of authority which the monarch of Great Britain would have shrunk from—an interference without precedent, against law, and against mercy."

Cooper was referring to the melancholy case of Jonathan Robbins. The English claimed that he had taken part in a mutiny on board a Royal Navy vessel. Adams accepted this claim and delivered Robbins to the English. "A case too little known, but of which the people ought to be fully apprized before the election, and they shall be." Cooper regarded the incident as a blemish on American law and a "great scandal."

Robbins was, or at least claimed to be, an American citizen impressed (taken by force) to serve on a Royal Navy vessel. A mutiny took place aboard the vessel, and Robbins disappeared. When he reappeared in Charleston two years later, he was arrested and held for extradition to Jamaica, a British possession, for trial. Following a provision of the Jay Treaty, Adams decided to turn him over to the British even though a move was under way in the Charleston federal court to hold a full hearing. Robbins, in British hands, was tried and convicted for mutiny. He was hanged.

Robbins's alleged mistreatment by Adams became a cause for the Republicans, to whom it proved that Adams had little use for proper judicial forms, for the separation of powers, and for the rights of American citizens. The entire episode made Adams look like a tool of the British, a perspective entirely unfair to Adams. In fact, Adams disliked Great Britain, distrusted its government, and was not a supporter of the Jay Treaty. But Cooper did not know Adams's mind, and, in any case, the temper of the times was so hot that Cooper's customary reserve was burned away. He concluded that Adams "had sanctioned the abolition of trial by jury in the Alien law, and entrenched his public character behind the legal barriers of the Sedition law."

Pickering may not have expected Cooper to step so unwittingly into the trap. When Adams was elected president, Cooper was not a prominent figure in the Republican propaganda machine. Cooper's paper was not one of the major Republican weeklies. His *Sunbury and Northumberland Gazette* had few subscribers. Published in western Pennsylvania from 1793, and only taken on by Cooper in 1794, it died a natural death in December 1800, after Cooper was jailed.

In general, Cooper's writings (excepting the broadside) hardly qualified for the categorization "false and malicious." They were not scurrilous or filled with untoward invective. Still something of an intellectual dilettante, he may not have understood the severity with which the Federalists intended to pursue their opponents. More an intellectual than a partisan, Cooper was a committed defender of free thinking and freedom of expression. His writings mixed satire and admonition in condemnation of Federalist policy. He portrayed himself as standing above party, a somewhat disingenuous pose, but if his depiction of the politics of the day was one-sided, it was also fairly mild compared to the vitriol that the more partisan editors and writers on both sides spilled.

Instead, Cooper used satire, parody, and other literary devices to amuse and edify his readers, though his tone could be barbed. It fit a genre of American literature — western humor — picaresque, sometimes written in dialect, respectful of no one and nothing. Typical was the language in which Cooper's Pennsylvania contemporary and fellow lawyer Hugh Henry Brackenridge described western law practice. Brackenridge's *Modern Chivalry* pilloried frontier lawyering:

> The profession of the law is a profitable business, where money is very easily got by the bare breath of the mouth. Nevertheless it requires time and study to qualify for this profession. Nay, the introduction to the study, by being put under an eminent lawyer in full practise, is itself very expensive. . . . [but] in a year's time he would learn to file a declaration; in another, to put in a plea; in a third, to join issue; and in a fourth, to conduct a trial; that unless a bill of exceptions had been filed, or there was a motion in arrest of judgment, or writ of error brought, he might be admitted the fifth, and begin to practice the sixth year: At all events, provided he would submit himself with due application to fasting, and cowskinning, and grinding plaster of Paris, pounding hemp, and picking

oakum, he might be a lawyer the seventh year, and wear spectacles like counsellor Grab, and take half a joe when he thought proper.

In 1800 Cooper published a series of his political essays from the *Northumberland Gazette* in an anthology aptly titled *Political Essays*. It evinced his learning, his picaresque sense of humor, and his genuine commitment to democracy. He made plain that he did not agree with mobs or rioters who violated the laws in western Pennsylvania, including those who would evade the payment of taxes. "If we are to enjoy the benefits of civil government, we must pay something for it." Obedience to the law was the very foundation of civil government. "It is hardly possible that any man of common understanding can be so ignorant as not to know that there must be an end to all government if laws enacted by constitutional authority are to be violently opposed wherever they are disliked." But a hint of his own politics crept into even this boilerplate defense of authority — he liked the Adams tax act because it was, in effect, a graduated tax. The rich man paid proportionally more than the poor man because the tax was on the value of a man's house. In a note, Cooper explained, "I inserted this [passage] not only to inculcate obedience to law, but to recommend particularly *This Principle of Taxation* here alluded to" (italics in original).

Politics was all the rage among the westerners when they gathered, and Cooper remarked on their manner of speech as well as their political preferences. "Everybody must have noticed something of [exaggeration] in the familiar phrases of common language; when some damned honest fellow, swears that the Madeira is devilish good . . . it is evident that these are incongruities of expression which nothing but the licence of colloquial familiarity could tolerate." But Cooper was also a moralizer. "These perversions of meaning are innocent; intended for no harm, they produce none; while the instances your correspondent complains of, are more serious." Politics was a more serious matter than drink.

By casting his political treatises as literary exercises, Cooper hoped to distance them from the more vindictive (and easily indicted) diatribes of the other Republican writers. But no politically literate reader could miss the message. He opened with a definition of political terms: "Democracy; the Government of the people: Democrat, a friend to the government of the people, in opposition to Monarchy, wherein one man claims the Government by hereditary right; and to Aristocracy, where a few persons arrogate the same privilege, to the exclusion of the people at large." The Republicans were the party of democracy.

> A constitution built upon the principle of the sovereignty of the people, and whose Rulers are chosen for limited period, by and at the will of the people? If such a government be not Democratic, I know not what is; nor can any citizen use the term democrat in this country as a term of reproach, without indirectly abusing the Constitution under which he lives, and which he has sworn to support [the last words a repetition of Bache's 1798 defiance of the Sedition Act].

To be sure, many among the Republicans had opposed the adoption of the Constitution in 1787. These were the anti-federalists. Cooper donned his scholar's gown again to explain why opposition to the Constitution in 1787 should not be equated with sedition in 1798.

> At the formation of the present Federal Constitution, there were (as may well be supposed) differences of opinion as to the principles of Union. The minority were termed Anti federalists on the occasion; the majority with Mr. Hamilton took the name of Federalists. But among the persons now termed Anti federal I have never an opinion, I have seen no publication, I know of no fact, which can authorize any man to believe, much less to assert, that they are [today] opposed to the Union whether as a party or individually.

In short, the anti-federalists had not only reconciled themselves to losing the ratification struggle, they had become earnest supporters of the federal government. "The [Anti federalists] are said to oppose the measures of Government, and this is given as proof of disaffection to the Union; but may not a man be well affected to the Union who disapproves of the British [i.e., the Jay] treaty, a French war, a standing army, or a navy to protect a few merchants in the carrying trade?"

One can read Cooper as the soul of moderation, even conciliation, in an era of fierce partisanship. "There certainly are violent men on both sides; there certainly are in this Country some men even of consequence who are savourers of monarchy; there may be others, too apt to think that the French Directory like the King of Great Britain can do no wrong. I hope such persons are few on either side." The real division among public men, in Cooper's opinion, was between

those who think the power of the Executive ought rather to be increased than diminished—who are fearful lest liberty should run into licentiousness, and would rather abridge than extend the rights of the people—who doubt about the practical expediency of a Republican Government, and begin to think a limited monarchy more tolerable than was heretofore supposed—who would strengthen the General at the expense of the State Governments, and stretch the meaning of the Federal Constitution to extend the powers of the President and Congress . . . such persons for the most part call themselves FEDERALISTS.

The Republicans, by contrast, were

cautious of entrusting or extending power unless evidently necessary to the happiness of the people . . . jealous of reposing unlimited confidence in persons of superior station . . . [those] who think, the public character of every public man a fair object of discussion, of praise or of censure   that restraint upon investigation like the late sedition laws, imply a dread of it . . . that a sincere friend to the Constitution and the Country may sometime disapprove the opinions and measures of the officers of Government.

This was a somewhat biased and not entirely fair characterization, but hardly a seditious libel. "I pretend not to be accurate myself when my authorities are so inaccurate in the use of the words. But I have attended pretty closely to parties here, and I know not where to find a better account than I have given. Your readers must judge for themselves."

Cooper opposed the passage of the Sedition Act. In the *Northumberland Gazette* and the *Political Essays* he argued that Congress had been barred from passing such an act by the First Amendment. Thus he well knew that the blast against Adams might bring trouble. It did.

When the Cooper broadside came to the attention of Pickering, he rushed it to Adams's attention. Pickering was part of the Hamilton wing of the Federalist Party, and thought Adams a little too lenient on the Republican opposition. He hoped to sting Adams's easily roused pride. As Pickering expected, Adams found the broadside to be "a meaner, more artful, or more malicious libel" than any of the more openly critical pieces of him or the government. "As far as it alludes to me, I despise it, but I have no doubt it is a libel against the whole government, and as such ought to be prosecuted." At Adams's behest, Pennsylvania federal attorney William Rawle arrested Cooper on April 9, and brought an indictment before a federal grand jury in Philadelphia on April 12, 1800. The grand jury found a true bill, and on April 16, 1800, the trial of Cooper for a seditious libel began in Philadelphia.

The circuit court met in the Supreme Court chamber, home to the city's municipal court in the town hall. It was a small chamber, with a raised bench set off from the counsel desks and the jury box. Behind the bench two grand windows let in sunlight. While it lacked grandeur, the room was serviceable and reasonably comfortable, though the chairs for the prosecution and defense lacked cushions and everyone had to raise their voices to be heard. Next door, along Chestnut Street, was Independence Hall, temporary home to Congress. In short, the setting was as close to the center of power as one could find in the new nation.

One would have assumed judicial impartiality in these paper wars, at least from reading John Adams's defense of an independent judiciary in his *Thoughts on Government* (1776): "The dignity and stability of government in all its branches, the morals of the people, and every blessing of society depend so much upon an upright and skillful administration of justice that the judicial power ought to be distinct from both the legislative and executive, and independent upon both, that so it may be a check upon both, as both should be checks upon that." But that was not the case. Recalling some years later his feelings about one of the Republican pamphlets, Justice Samuel Chase told the House of Representatives that it was "a heinous offense" that "excited disgust and indignation in every breast not wholly depraved."

On the bench, Justice Chase sat with district court judge Richard Peters. The federal system was divided into districts and Chase rode circuit, sitting with Peters often when the middle circuit court met in Philadelphia. Chase would later be tarred with the sobriquet of "the American Jeffreys," a reference to the English high court justice George Jeffreys, who, ignoring defendants' legal rights, summarily tried, demanded the conviction of, and ordered the hanging of hundreds of suspected rebels in 1685.

But Chase was no George Jeffreys. Deeply religious, conservative in habits of mind, a Maryland anti-federalist who changed his mind in time for President Washington to appoint him to the High Court in 1796, he was a no-nonsense figure on the bench, and rebuked counsel when he felt they had offended him, the court, or the law. In fact, Adams never fully trusted Chase, writing to Abigail when Chase was nominated for the High Court that Chase had "a mist" of "suspicion and impurity" in his character. But Chase campaigned for Adams in 1796, and as the trial unfolded, Chase would reveal that he viewed with asperity Cooper's assault on the president's character.

Peters by contrast was far more professional on the bench, serving as federal judge from 1791 until his death in 1828. A longtime resident of the Philadelphia area, he was early a Whig in the revolutionary crisis, was elected to the Continental Congress as a member from Pennsylvania and later to the state legislature, and helped reestablish ties between the American Episcopal Church and the Church of England after the war. Peters, like Cooper, was a man of many parts, including an interest in farming. He even published a report of the uses of gypsum, or "plaster of paris," by farmers (far less jocularly than Brackenridge's references). Peters saw this as a contribution to "useful knowledge" and dedicated the 1797 pamphlet to George Washington, whom Peters knew had an interest in "agricultural improvements." Respected by leaders of both parties for his mild temperament and his knowledge of the law, he was never accused of the partisan rancor that Chase so often exhibited.

To better understand the way in which Justice Chase and Judge Peters viewed Cooper's trial, why they thought Cooper's scribbling was of great seriousness, one must remember that in these days incendiary words had already led to violent deeds. Three times, during Shays's rebellion in western Massachusetts (1786–1787), the Whiskey Rebellion in western Pennsylvania and Maryland (1793–1794), and

Fries's Rebellion (1798–1799), rioters had attacked the government officials in the course of their duty.

Only a year before they heard Cooper's case the two men sat on the bench in the treason trials arising from Fries's Rebellion. The Federalist plan for war with France required funding. (Jefferson's repeated denunciation of expensive government was a criticism directed at Federalist plans to raise money for the war.) The Federalists passed a tax on homes, which Pennsylvania residents opposed. Some of these opponents were German immigrants, and, led by Jacob Fries, they violently resisted the collection of the tax. Fries and two others were tried for treason and convicted, with Chase telling the jury that they were guilty. Five of Fries's coconspirators were convicted of violating the conspiracy provision of the Sedition Act on May 15, 1799. They were fined and sent to prison. Adams would pardon Fries and the other two, sparing them the death penalty. Everyone in the courtroom at Cooper's trial knew that words might lead to sticks and stones.

What was Cooper thinking as he stood before the bench that morning? He knew he had little hope of success. According to the Sedition Act, truth was a defense against the charges. Some of what Cooper said in the broadside was certainly true. But much of it was opinion. Opinion based on fact might be allowed as true under a lenient rule, but Chase had already said that he intended to instruct the jury in the older English civil libel rule, that every statement must be proved true in all its particulars. Cooper, trained in English law, knew the rule well, and knew he could not prove everything he wrote to be a matter of fact.

But the Jeffersonian scribblers were not without a weapon of their own. They kept careful account of their woes and published them. Reports of the sedition trials published after the fact included the speeches of the defendants, but, as these were supposedly factual, they might (in theory) not provide fodder for a second round of indictments. (In fact, a few of the federal prosecutors did seek indictments against already convicted writers for what they published while in prison.)

Cooper arranged for the publication of a verbatim account of his trial. One can see in it extravagance on both sides, as the defendant and the prosecution, the latter aided by the bench, sought to make this prosecution a "show trial." Indeed, a published account of his trial—

as a restatement of his political opinions – was never far from his thinking as he conducted his own defense. Doing this allowed him to read into the record a reprise of his criticisms of the Adams administration. One cannot be sure that Cooper's transcription of what was said is totally accurate. It depended upon stenographic notes, and these at their best omit material, condense material, and may even slant material. Nevertheless, a careful reading of the trial records, and a comparison of this account with other accounts of trials under the Sedition Act, suggests that Cooper wanted to be accurate.

Chase probably recognized that Cooper intended to publish the account, and he curbed his own tongue accordingly. After all, in his *Political Essays* Cooper had taken note of Chase's own reluctance to proceed against Bache under a common law indictment. The two men did not know one another intimately, but they had already taken the measure of one another. Thus a wary Chase did not want to give free rein to Cooper's sharp wit. The justice nevertheless allowed Cooper great license. It is also possible that Chase hoped Cooper would say something violating the act in the course of his defense of himself and publish the same.

Letting Cooper go on and on might give Cooper enough rope to hang himself. How?

Cooper might commit contempt of court. Disrespect directed to the bench or overt disobedience to an order from the bench was contempt of court. The judges' discretion in contempts was almost unlimited. This was why Cooper, when the time came for him to speak, wanted to use quotations from the Federalist newspapers and testimony from Federalists in court rather than offer his own opinions.

Perhaps anyone supporting Cooper might fall into another trap. Today, lawyers in court are free to make accusations or offer characterizations during a trial that elsewhere might be grounds for libel suits. What lawyers say about a case or the parties to it on the courthouse steps, however, is not privileged (i.e., protected against libel suits). Reporters who quote the lawyer, and newspapers or other media sources that repeat the quotation, may also be liable to contempt citations. Cooper's friends might find themselves in this snare.

The trial began with the reading of the grand jury indictment. The jurors had found a "true bill." Grand juries might also find "no bill," in which case the prosecution ended. The grand jury only needed to decide, by a majority vote, that there was probable cause to try Cooper. Some grand juries are the tools of the prosecution, for the prosecution has control of the evidence presented to them. But a fair reading of the broadside and the statute suggests that an unbiased grand juror might have voted a true bill.

Cooper had given the court a $1,000 bail bond, as had Israel Israel, esq., to ensure Cooper's appearance at trial if the grand jury voted a true bill. Israel was elected high sheriff of Philadelphia and served from 1800 to 1803. Philadelphia had a small but highly active Sephardic Jewish population, including bankers, merchants, and lawyers such as Israel and Bache's counsel Moses Levy. Some had come from New York City in 1776, when it was occupied by British forces. During the war, Israel was the head of the city's committee of safety and a leader in the Jewish community. His word was as good as his bond. Israel was a cosurety to Cooper, his bond a promise that he would insure that Cooper appeared. Other Republican writers had already gone into hiding. For example, James Duane was hiding out somewhere in Philadelphia.

When the trial court convened on the 16th of April, William Rawle, federal attorney in the district, read in court the indictment that he had prepared for the grand jury's deliberation. Rawle was a Quaker whose family were loyalists during the Revolution. A superbly able and fair lawyer, he was a moderate Federalist and resigned his prosecutorial office after the Cooper trial. But for the previous half decade in service as federal attorney, Rawle had been a busy man. He was the prosecutor of the so-called Whiskey Rebels after a gang of western Pennsylvania farmers and tradesmen refused to pay the excise tax on distilled spirits. (They did a little more than refuse to pay: they attacked the tax collectors. After they were tried and convicted, President Washington commuted the sentences of the two ringleaders tried for treason.) Rawle had also prosecuted the tax resisters in Fries's Rebellion. Again Rawle got convictions.

The grand inquest of the United States of America [the federal grand jury] in and for the district of Pennsylvania . . . do present, that Thomas Cooper, late of the district of Pennsylvania, attorney at law being a person of a wicked and turbulent disposition design- ing and intending to defame the President of the United States, and to bring him into contempt and disrepute, and to excite against him the hatred of the good people of the United States, on the 2nd of November, 1799, in the district aforesaid, and within the jurisdiction of this court, wickedly and maliciously did write, print and publish a false, scandalous and malicious writing against the said President of the United States.

To wit, the broadside.

Some of the language in the indictment was formulaic, dating back to a time in English history when crimes against the state supposedly brought down the wrath of heaven. Rawle likely did not think Cooper wicked in the sense of being sinful. "Wicked" meant that Cooper had acted voluntarily and knowingly. The intention to violate the law was one of the elements of the offense the prosecution had to prove. The same formula brought "malicious" into the indictment. Malice meant harm. Rawle had to prove that the writing harmed the government, that is, in some way hobbled its ability to perform or leant impetus to those who would commit sedition.

Cooper's account of the trial reported his response. "To this bill of indictment Mr. Cooper put in the plea of not guilty, and also pleaded the truth of the facts in justification [as allowed in the act]." Next came the surprise. "He directed subpoenas to be issued for the President of the United States, for Timothy Pickering Esq Jacob Wagner, (a clerk in Timothy Pickering's office,) and John Davenport Esqr. Member of Congress." Cooper wanted to make a point. No one was above the law, certainly not elected officials. In England, two civil wars, a series of declarations of rights by Parliament, and three dynastic shifts were required before the Crown set aside its claims to rule by divine right. The Revolution, the Constitution, and the First Amendment together announced that President John Adams was not above the law. If the law, in particular the Judiciary Act and Process Act of 1789, were binding on every party to a case, then a defendant had a legal right to ask a court to compel evidence from relevant parties.

But what evidence could John Adams give that would aid Cooper's case? Did Cooper propose to cross-examine the president? What a spectacle that would have been. And not impossible—because Adams lived and worked within a short walk of the courthouse. As for members of Congress:

Previous to directing the subpoenas, [Cooper] stated to the court, that he understood it had been customary . . . that when a member of the Legislature was intended to be subpoenaed during session, for the court from whence the subpoena issued, to write to the Speaker of the House requesting that the House would permit the process to be served. If that were the practice, Mr. Cooper begged the court would be pleased to conform to it in the present instance.

In other words, he challenged Chase to issue the subpoenas compelling the attendance of Cooper's prospective witnesses.

Here began a familiar stage play, a performance of legal procedure that is part of every major trial. But these lines were not scripted. It was improvisation, a riff on conventional criminal trial tactics that Cooper played. The drama would turn out to have three acts, a prologue, and a concluding speech as the play ran its course.

Judge Chase responded to Cooper's motion. He did not want to invent his own lines for this prologue: "I know of no such practice and no such privilege. I do not know that any such privilege is given by the Constitution, and if it be not given there, I cannot give it. I do not like setting precedent of this nature." But he was constrained as well by rules. "The court will do its duty, and direct process to be issued upon any man whatever his situation may be, if the law does not exempt him from it." At this moment Cooper might have found Chase's dilemma amusing. Surely the justice did not. "I shall certainly write no such letter," he bristled. But how could he do his "duty" and refuse to issue the subpoenas? It was a real moment of high drama of the sort that may suddenly occur in any highly visible trial. In fact, Pickering would attend — he would not have missed it for the world. He is even reported to have joined Chase and Peters on the bench.

Recognizing that Chase teetered on the brink of professional misconduct, Rawle had the temerity to admonish the justice. "I believe Sir, the practice has been to apply in that manner. I believe the Judges of the supreme court of this state [that is, Pennsylvania] after deliberation, determined on the expediency of proceeding in that way to avoid giving occasion for any dispute on the subject."

Rawle was referring to what would become known as the "Virginia rule." It would become the centerpiece in the Sedition Act trial of James Callender later that year in Virginia. Chase presided over it.

Callender's counsel would argue, to no avail, that process in the federal circuit court must follow Virginia's process. The rule derived from the Judiciary Act of 1789 and the Process Act of 1789. It was simple: federal courts would apply the procedural rules of the states in which they sat, unless a federal procedural rule took precedence. (Federal equity rules, for example, took precedence over state equity rules in certain kinds of civil cases.) Judge Peters, also from Pennsylvania, and like Rawle appalled by Chase's blanket refusal to follow the rules, added: "When I was the Speaker of a single Legislature, I have had letters of that kind addressed to me of a similar purpose."

Alexander Dallas, in court as Cooper's unofficial counsel (and to record the proceedings), joined the conversation. He was no friend of Chase and perhaps enjoyed the chance to pour salt in what was becoming a gaping wound:

> I beg leave to suggest to the court, that the practice of writing to the Speaker in such a case was adopted to avoid the difficulty that might arise from the clashing of justifications. If subpoenas were served on a member of the Legislature during session, and he did not choose to attend, the next process of the court (if prayed for,) must be attachment; and attachment cannot be enforced without arrest: But the members of the Legislature are privileged from arrest during session.

Chase, confronted with authority contrary to his own inclinations, bulled his way forward. He ignored Rawle and Peters and directed his remarks to Dallas:

> Sir, the court thank you for your suggestion as Amicus Curiae [friend of the court, a mischaracterization of Dallas's role] but we should take care to avoid this clashing of justifications. If the member subpoenaed during the session would not attend, we would issue no attachment, we would put off the cause till his attendance could be compelled. Mr. Cooper may take out his subpoenas; we shall write no such letter.

Peters, wishing to avoid an open confrontation with Chase, backpedaled: "I wish it to be understood that in my opinion, no such process ought to issue to members of the Legislature during session; for I do not approve of issuing process which we cannot enforce."

Cooper was allowed to depart the court to prepare his defense. The prologue of the trial had ended.

CHAPTER 5

Freedom of the Press on Trial

Act one of the trial proper began with "Mr. Cooper . . . coming into the court on Wednesday morning (the time appointed for bringing on the trial,) [and] enquir[ing] if his subpoenas had been served, and particularly the subpoena directed to the President of the United States." Cooper wanted to embarrass the administration, at the very least by showing how its leaders refused to obey the law. Chase was still adamant. He told Cooper "the clerk of the court showed us your directions to him, to subpoena the President of the United States, and we directed him not to issue the subpoena; we thought the proceeding very improper."

Chase had allowed Cooper to file the paperwork with the clerk, knowing that the clerk (another Federalist appointee) would ask Chase whether the court could issue the subpoenas, and Chase planned to say no all the time. By his directing Cooper to seek the attendance of witnesses by subpoena, then refusing to issue the writs (recall that Chase also refused to summon the witnesses himself), Cooper was left without anyone to examine. He could not prove the truth of his assertions by his own words. Thus he might as well plead guilty.

Cooper would not give up so easily. "Will the court have the goodness to hear me on that question?" Chase, amusing himself, let out a little more rope. "Certainly Sir; go on." Cooper minded his manners. On the one hand, his request was a ploy. Adams had nothing to say that would aid Cooper's case. On the other hand, the issue was of great moment. Would the court actually say that the president was not subject to subpoena? "I did not expect (may it please the court) that any objection would have been made to issuing this process to procure the attendance of the President. It is the duty of every good citizen for the furtherance of justice, to give his testimony when duty called upon for that purpose by the process of a court of justice." Was the president above the law? Did the Constitution exempt him from giving testimony or appearing in court?

Could the court have enforced a subpoena on the president of the United States? Would this have violated separation of powers? Would failure to issue the subpoena suggest that the president was above the law? Even if Cooper's purpose were merely dilatory and frivolous, did he not have a right to ask for the subpoena, and did the court's refusal to "write the letter" not amount to a dereliction of its duty as a court of law?

In 1807, before the trial of Aaron Burr for treason commenced, Burr asked Chief Justice John Marshall, presiding over the circuit court, to subpoena certain papers from President Thomas Jefferson. Initially, Jefferson was reluctant to supply them. After some icy correspondence with Marshall, Jefferson offered to copy the correspondence Burr wanted to see and provide it to Marshall. Jefferson cordially hated Marshall, but complied. In *U.S. v. Nixon* (1974), a unanimous U.S. Supreme Court ordered President Richard Nixon to turn over to the federal district court a number of Oval Office tape recordings that were material to the Watergate investigation. In *Clinton v. Jones* (1997), another unanimous U.S. Supreme Court ruled that the president has no privilege to ignore a subpoena in a civil matter during his tenure in office.

Cooper was two hundred years ahead of his time. "Before I determined on applying for this subpoena, I examined (as it was my duty to do) the Constitution of the United States, to discover if any privilege of exemption from this process was given to the President by that Constitution, I could find none." Cooper then chided Chase: "I was glad to hear the opinion of your Honour that you would not undertake to confer privileges which the Constitution had not granted. If no such exemption then can be claimed in your opinion by any member of our Legislature, why should it be assumed by the President if the Constitution does not give him this privilege of exemption? I may claim the subpoena as matter of rights."

Cooper next essayed an argument similar to one in Gallatin's address to the House on July 10. A logical conundrum, but here almost picaresque:

There is a farther and peculiar reason in this cause, why the President even if he had this privilege should not claim it as against myself. If I call him into this court, who compels me to do it? Himself. . . . The publication for which I am indicted is not a voluntary effusion, it was forced from me — I was compelled to write it in vindication of my own character, grossly and falsely attacked in consequence of a disclosure on the part of the President, of what I cannot but deem private correspondence.

Adams had only himself to blame for telling Pickering about Cooper's request for the judicial appointment. Actually, as secretary of state, Pickering was supposed to prepare and sign all federal appointments. But Cooper could not resist the sly whack at the president. And in itself, it was not a seditious libel.

Chase no doubt felt the underlying insult to his integrity and was not amused.

We have heard you Sir: patiently; and in consideration of your being without counsel [as if Dallas had dematerialized and Cooper were not licensed to practice law]. We have permitted you to say what we would not have suffered any counsel to advance: Sir, we consider your situation but you have totally mistaken the whole business. It is not upon the objection of privilege that we have refused this subpoena: This court will do its duty against any man however elevated his situation may be. — You have mistaken the ground. — We are of opinion that in the case of a prosecution for a libel tending to bring the President of the United States into contempt, he cannot be compelled to appear at all.

Why not? one might muse. The indictment had not come from the president. It came from the judicial branch. (Of course, everyone in court knew that Adams had ordered Rawle to seek it.) But there was another, far more subtle issue here. Cooper was arguing that Adams could not be a judge in his own cause. Attempts to do this by the King of England had led to the English Civil Wars of the 1640s. Chase again simply bulled through the niceties of Cooper's argument. "What, shall you bring the President on such a prosecution, into this court to prove your charges to ask him . . . 'were you guilty of malad-ministration?' Sir this cannot be permitted, and if you had been a lawyer you would not have made the request." In fact, however, Hay, Nicholas, and Dallas would all make it at one time or another in ser-vice of their clients at trials over which Chase presided. And Chase knew that Cooper was a lawyer and practiced law in Pennsylvania.

Cooper would not be bullied. "I have great deference for the opin-ion of the Court, but this is a new point: will the Court be good enough to hear me upon it?" Chase, either knowing that the law was not on his side or not caring because he had already taken sides, replied, "No Sir; the court will not hear you after they have give[n] their decision: It was a very improper and a very indecent request." Cooper risked a citation for contempt by continuing, but he did: "I assure the Court, I am not guilty of intentional impropriety. But a pre-liminary question . . . arose between Mr. Rawle and me not connected with the substance of the indictment: cannot I have the benefit of the President's testimony on that question?" Cooper was dragging Rawle into the conversation. After all, Rawle had already corrected Chase. The justice shot back, "No Sir; [Adams] cannot be brought here at all upon this Trial. Are you ready to proceed?"

The first scene of act one ended quietly. Cooper conceded, "I believe Sir, I shall be."

Scene two of act one began when the trial jury was called, but before they were sworn Cooper raised the very same issue that Chase had ruled upon at the end of the first day.

Mr. Cooper suggested to the court that some of the passages charged in the indictment were grounded upon a certain address to the President in the summer of one thousand seven hundred and ninety-eight, and the answers thereto; that he had applied to Mr. Rawle to admit as evidence of those documents, the publications of them in the common newspapers; that he meant to use [Feder-alist publisher John] Fenno's paper [*Gazette of the United States*] for the purpose; that Mr. Rawle at first consented, but had since writ-ten him a note retracting that assent.

That is, Rawle had been willing to let Cooper read the Pickering piece into the record, then either changed his mind or was told not to allow it in evidence. Cooper sensed that this was another fissure in (what he supposed to be) collusion between prosecution and bench, and he wanted it exposed.

Cooper's request was not on point — the indictment specified only his broadside of November 1799. But if Cooper could get the Federalist paper into the record, along with his comment on it, he could make a case that he was merely defending his own honor against a biased and unfair newspaper article, rather than libeling the administration.

In 1800, the law of evidence governing what was admissible as evidence in a court of law stood at a critical juncture. In earlier times, hearsay and rumor, documentary evidence that one party could not produce or the other party could not see in advance, could all be entered at trial. Whatever the judge allowed a party to say or to produce was admissible. But all that was changing, and changing fast. New English treatises on evidence were laying down rules that told lawyers and judges what evidence to admit and what to bar. The best evidence was what was written at the time of the incident and could be produced in court in its original form. Copies of Fenno's papers were not the best evidence of Adams's conduct — Adams's own testimony would have been better. But the Federalist press was the best evidence that Cooper could offer.

Cooper, trained in law in England, may have known something of the evolving law of evidence. Ironically, Chase may not have been so well versed as Cooper on the newest developments in the admissibility of documents. Given this possibility, Cooper may have been chiding Chase for his condescending remarks about Cooper's lack of expertise. Chase may have seen through the ruse and resented Cooper's effrontery. But whatever either man knew or intended, Chase could not simply dismiss Cooper's point. If Cooper could not produce any evidence, what was the purpose of the trial? By definition, a trial was an attempt to ascertain matters of fact. That is why triers of fact — the jury — sat in the box. Chase ran in place: "When the question comes before us we will consider it. In the mean time you must go on your own way and judge for yourself. But, Mr. Rawle, what objection have you to admit the news-papers to be read (that is so far as they are relevant to the question,) if you have no reason to suspect their accuracy?"

Rawle might have asked himself if Chase was trying to be fair. Or did he take pleasure in chiding Rawle, for the temerity of his earlier correction of the bench? Rawle: "I beg leave to state to the court, that on Mr. Cooper's applying to me on this subject. I at first consented, but afterwards I retracted that consent for the reasons assigned in the following letter." Rawle had written:

Upon further consideration of the request you made to me this morning as to admitting the printed addresses to, and answers for the President of the United States on your trial, I am apprehensive some inconvenience may result from it as it is impossible for me to be certain whether inaccuracy in some instances or design in others, may not have rendered the printed accounts unfaithful transcripts of the originals.

Rawle was quibbling. A copy of the printed newspaper was surely the best possible evidence of what had appeared in the newspaper. Was Cooper going to counterfeit newspapers? Rawle had reconsidered because he belatedly realized what Chase knew all along. These trials were all about politics and political posturing. Putting Fenno's venom into the record made Cooper's publication look tame. Even so, it was embarrassing. To Cooper, Rawle apologized: "I trust that so short a space of time has elapsed since our communication that no inconvenience to you will result from it, but should it be the case I shall make no opposition to a commensurate prolongation of the time previous to the trial, so that you may be as fully prepared as if the conversation of this morning had not taken place."

Judge Peters was bewildered. In truth the bizarre exchange among Cooper, Chase, and Rawle seemed to have no focus. "It is quite time enough for us to decide this question when it come regularly before us," Peters offered. But it had already come before the court. When was a better time to decide the admissibility of the Federalist prints? Cooper pressed his tiny advantage. "If that be the case I must not in point of prudence subject myself to the hazard of being deprived of a most material part of my testimony. . . . Yet I must run no risk: I therefore pray the court to defer the trial until I can procure office copies." Chase: "Will you be ready on Saturday Sir?" Cooper: "If I can procure the copies I shall." Chase: "Sir that is not the question. If your evidence is not ready we shall judge of that, then." Mr. Cooper: "I shall be ready on Saturday." Act one was done, leaving the players a little worse for wear, observers confused, and the issue in a little more suspense than when Rawle read the indictment.

The second act curtain rose on April 19 at 9 o'clock. Cooper made an opening statement. He was an attorney and represented himself. Why he did not avail himself of Dallas's services remains unclear, but Bache had bankrupted himself by employing counsel, as would Callender until he found wealthy Virginia Republican backers. The Federalists knew well that the Republican editors were not well-heeled and that hiring counsel could empty their pockets even before they were found guilty and fined. Thus the prosecutions could begin what conviction, fines, and imprisonment would finish—breaking the Republican press.

In any case, Cooper was competent to represent himself. Chase's earlier slur that Cooper's motion to summon Adams showed the defendant's incompetence was gratuitous and incorrect, as the debate over admissibility had proved. At any rate, Cooper was persistent. "The Court may perhaps remember the proposals I made to the Attorney General [Cooper meant Rawle] respecting some public documents, which I meant to give in evidences. They were published in a news-paper wherein all the acts of government were usually inserted. . . . In conformity to this expectation, I have endeavored to procure those copies without delay." The trial was moving swiftly. "Much of the supposed libel is founded on expressions contained in certain addresses to the President in the summer on one thousand seven hundred and ninety-eight, and his answers thereto." This was not the broadside, but the original account of the rendition of Robbins. Cooper had a defense if he could prove through these documents the truth of what he said of Adams a year later. Or so he claimed. But the libel was not the truth of the Robbins case, it was Cooper's denunciation of Adams's conduct in the matter. Had Cooper merely described what Adams did (turning over Robbins without waiting for trial in the federal court) and then said that Adams violated the law one suspects that the grand jurors might have voted no bill on the indictment.

If the court would not allow the introduction of the newspapers, perhaps official copies would serve? Cooper "applied by letter to the Secretary of State [Pickering], who returned for answer the next morning that there were none of those addresses or answers deposited in his office." Reasonable, one supposes, for the secretary of state had a clerk and a filing cabinet — hardly enough space for an archive of correspondence — but Cooper was undaunted. "On receiving this information I sent directly the following note to the President. . . . 'Being indicted for a supposed Libel in the circuit court of the United States now sitting in Philadelphia, I find it necessary to apply for official copies of the papers of which I transmit an enclosed list.'" Not surprisingly, neither Pickering nor Adams was cooperative. "I applied yesterday afternoon to the Secretary of State, who has just now sent me word they are not to be found in his office," Cooper told the president; "I beg therefore that your Excellency would have the goodness to direct your secretary to make them out for most expeditiously as possible, and to accept of the present application as legal notice of my request." What bravado! Adams did not reply.

Cooper continued his tale. "The next morning, conceiving there was a mode of expediting the business, I sent my son to purchase a book purposing to be 'A selection of addresses and answers to and from the President of the United States in the year one thousand seven hundred and ninety eight,'" which Cooper then sent to Adams with a note. "'Mr. Cooper presents his respects to Mr. Shaw [Adams's secretary] and being desirous of saving time and trouble, takes the liberty of suggesting whether the collection of addresses and answers herewith sent, might not be collated with the originals, and then copies would only be necessary of those wanted by Mr. Cooper, which the volume does not contain.'" Cooper reported the results: "Mr. Shaw returned the following answer: 'Mr. Shaw informs Mr. Cooper; that he will not receive any information concerning answers to addresses from this house.'"

Chase had to be impressed or at least amused. "I suppose you mean the President's house? Was he there at that time?"

"Mr. Cooper: He was at the President's house — Under the circumstances I have related, I do not think it possible for me falsely to go on, while the person who may fairly be considered in some degree as my prosecutor, holds in his possession the legal evidence on which I must rest my defence."

Cooper made one concession, more to Rawle than to Chase.

Nor indeed is Fenno's paper quite accurate, for in a collated copy, procured for me by Colonel Lyon [Matthew Lyon, "Colonel" being a title that revolutionary officers affected] from the office of the Secretary of War, I find manuscript corrections, altho' they are not very material. . . . I presume there is the same law for Mr. Rawle as for me, and as he objected to the production of news-paper evidence in the first instance, so may I, on the same grounds; therefore I move the court to put off the trial until I can procure the papers required.

The recital anticipated the conversation of the lawyers in the fictitious case of *Jarndyce v. Jarndyce*, at the opening of Charles Dickens's *Bleak House*, where "a large advocate with great whiskers, a little voice, and an interminable brief . . . mistily engaged in one of the ten thousand stages of an endless cause" amidst the gray herd of pleaders at the bar "tripping one another up on slippery precedents, groping knee deep in technicalities," adding a fog of words to the fog that shrouded the city.

Chase, a choleric, stout man, must have colored red in the face as he denied this motion. Whether Cooper was stalling or simply pettifogging, his tactics were taking a toll on Chase's rapidly dwindling supply of patience. "You are mistaken in supposing the prosecutor of this indictment is the President of the United States. It is no such thing — It is at the suit of the United States you are indicted, for publishing a false scandalous and malicious libel, with intent to defame the President of the United States."

Chase saw a lawsuit as a wager and lectured Cooper: "Your mistakes must fall on yourself. . . . You must take the chance. . . . Nor had you a right to make these assertions unless you had proof that would bear you out in them." If Cooper did not have the evidence at hand when he wrote, he should not have published his thoughts.

If in making [your] assertions you relied on the public paper it was at your own risk; and it was your own fault not to have had authentic copies. You think that you have a right to obtain official copies of what may be necessary for your Defence, you are greatly mistaken. No law that I know of, authorizes you to require them, and I see no reason why the proper officers should give copies.

Chase then lectured Cooper on the duties of a good citizen. "You suppose that the offices of government ought to be open to your inspection—it is not so." If any defendant could go on fishing expeditions through the records of government, the government could not perform its official duties. Cooper had worn Chase's patience paper thin. "Even if you had these copies the court would determine on their admissibility as evidence. If you offer newspapers, the court will determine whether they can be given in as evidence or not. . . . But do not take it for granted that you may examine witnesses or produce evidence that has nothing to do with the cause." True enough, the court would rule on the relevance of any evidence, and on its probative value (versus its prejudicial impact). But here the court would not even aid Cooper in gaining the evidence.

Denied the assistance of the court and the assent of the executive branch, Cooper pronounced his own judgment on the question of evidence. "Since the court is of opinion that I cannot produce this evidence, which I consider as material to my Defence, and as I am not fully prepared for trial, expecting that I could obtain this evidence, I wish the trial to be put off on other grounds."

Chase replied with the stock answer: "If you can show good grounds the court will consent to put it off," as if there were any good grounds in his mind. Cooper had one more request. He had "subpoenaed several members of the Legislature, but I am apprehensive they deem it inconsistent with their duty to attend. . . . If they do not, I fear I cannot go on." Chase asked the marshal if he had subpoenaed the witnesses. He had. They were Pickering, Robert Goodloe Harper, a Federalist congressman from Maryland, Gallatin, Edward Livingston, Matthew Lyon, and three others. Pickering and Harper were there, ready to defend the administration. Republicans Livingston, Lyon, and Gallatin were absent. A subpoena may be delivered to an address. Lyon was making himself scarce, as a new indictment of him was already voted. Livingston was at his family estate on the Hudson River. But Gallatin lived in Philadelphia and would soon arrive at the door of the court. An honest and loyal friend to Cooper, he would by his presence at the very least lend moral support.

But Chase warned Cooper that he must first satisfy the court that the evidence the witnesses were to give before the jury would "justify you." In short, before Cooper questioned the witnesses, he must tell the court what they would say. The evidence must be relevant and pro-bative. Chase offered Cooper the chance to swear in an affidavit that the witnesses had something material to contribute to Chase's defense. But Cooper's defense was that his remarks were true. None of the witnesses could offer more than their own opinion about Cooper's publication. They could no more prove his characterization of Adams's behavior true (or false for that matter) than he could.

Cooper nevertheless provided the affidavit, after which, predictably, Chase ruled: "This affidavit is not sufficient; you do not state your reasons why you believe they are material witnesses." Chase then added one more insult to the injury: "As you are without Counsel the court will show you more indulgence. Had Counsel offered this affidavit we should not allow any explanatory affidavit to be made, but we shall allow you to make one. Therefore take time for your affidavit."

An unexpected turn of events closed the second act of the performance. As Cooper prepared the affidavit, "Judge Chase (after some conversation with a gentleman near him) said 'I am inclined to think the witnesses will all attend. Therefore call them; I am informed that they will all attend. Mr. Harper and Mr. Gallatin were in court, we had better send for them. We must no doubt pay attention to the conveniences of the house [of representatives].'" Who was near enough to Chase to catch his ear, and important enough for Chase to listen? Likely it was Harper, close to Chase in more ways than one. For Harper was as stern and committed a Federalist as Chase and a superb lawyer to boot.

Judge Peters interjected, "If the gentlemen will voluntarily appear, it is well; if not, we cannot compel them."

Chase told the marshal, "Go and ask them if it is convenient to attend."

Peters added, "I have seen several of them. They will attend. The officer says they will attend."

Cooper was wrong-footed by the sudden appearance of his witnesses. He never expected them. Chase had called Cooper's bluff. "If that be the case I have no objection; but as I did not expect my trial to commence this morning, my papers are not here. Will the court permit me to go for them?" Apparently, Cooper's request for subpoenas for members of Congress had been a ploy all along. Perhaps he really did not know what to ask them. After all, the indictment turned on Adams's diplomacy, a matter with which they had little to do. What could they say? Still, the court permitted Cooper to rush home and return with his "papers."

Act three began with Cooper back at the defense table. The motions part of the trial had ended, and Rawle began the case for the prosecution. Rawle opened "by observing that the Defendant stands charged with attempts which the practice and policy of all civilized nations has thought it right all times to punish with severity; with having published a false scandalous and malicious attack on the character of the President of the United States with an intent to excite the hatred and contempt of the people of this country against the man of their choice."

Rawle affected to be bewildered why Cooper, who had so much for which to be grateful, had turned on the very country that offered him asylum. The same argument was a staple in the Federalists' defense of the Alien Friends Act. Cooper was not the only one who listened to the House debates on the bills. "It was much to be lamented that every person who had a tolerable facility at writing should think he had a right to attack and overset those authorities and officers whom the people of this country had thought fit to appoint." Rawle also treated Cooper to a lesson on the good citizen's conduct. "Nor was it to be endured that foul and infamous falsehoods should be uttered and published with impunity against the President of the United States, whom the people themselves had placed in that high office, and in which he has acted with so much credit to himself and benefit to them."

Most of this was political rhetoric rather than legal argument, but cast as offended dignity rather than partisanship. It was vital to rouse the jury's sense of indignation at Cooper's scribbling. The prosecution must not seem to be partisan itself. "It was a sense of public duty that called for this prosecution. It was necessary that an example should be made to deter others from misleading the people by such false and defamatory publications." Cooper was to be that example, for his was the first of a planned series of trials of lesser figures. The jury must understand that although Cooper was indicted for a single publication and a single set of accusations against Adams, he could not be let off with a warning. "Being of the profession of the law [a fact that Chase had ignored], a man of education and literature, [Cooper] availed himself of those advantages for the purpose of disseminating his dangerous productions in a remote part of the country where he had gained influence." What was more, "it was high time for the law to interfere and restrain the libelous spirit which had been so long permitted to extend itself against the highest and most deserving characters." "High time" meant election time.

Rawle also explained why words could do such damage. To abuse the men with whom the public has entrusted the management of their national concern, to withdraw from them the confidence of the people so necessary for conducting the public business, was in direct opposition to the duties of a good citizen. No matter that Cooper's paper appeared in an insular and isolated part of the back country.

Mischief of this kind were to be dreaded in proportion as the country around [rural areas such as Northumberland County, Pennsylvania] is less informed, and a man of sense and education has it more in his power to extend the mischief which he is inclined to propagate. . . . Error leads to discontent, discontent to a fancied idea of oppression, and that to insurrection, of which the two instances, which had already happened, were alarming proofs, and well known to the jury.

Rawle's reference to insurrection was understood by everyone sitting in the jury box. In 1793–1794, Northumberland was the scene of widespread protest against Alexander Hamilton and the Federalists' excise taxes in the so-called Whiskey Rebellion (because the tax fell on distilled spirits, and farmers in western Pennsylvania distilled the grains they could not send to market). Federal tax collectors were beaten and driven from the region. President Washington assembled an armed force of 10,000 men (with Hamilton as his second in command), and Hamilton led the force to the area. The rebels surrendered. Tried and convicted in federal court, they were then pardoned by Washington. But the passions of that day still remained high.

Scene two of the third act opened with Cooper's address to the jury. He was earnest, for the address was his last chance to escape jail and fines.

[If] I have been guilty of publishing with the basest motives a foul and infamous libel on the character of the President; of exciting against him the hatred and contempt of the people of this country, by gross and malicious falsehoods — then indeed would it be his [that is, Adams's; though the indictment and trial was not an executive action, Cooper wished to portray it as such] duty to bring me before this Tribunal, it would be yours to convict, and the duty of the court to punish me. But I hope in the course of this trial, I shall be enabled to prove to your satisfaction that I have published nothing which truth will not justify.

Truth and "honest and fair" motives were Cooper's defense.

His imposing brow furrowed, and his fine, almost delicate eyes fixed on the jury, Cooper displayed the professorial manner that would mark his later life. He rejected overblown courtroom rhetoric. The most famous trial lawyers at that time in America, including Hamilton, William Wirt, Luther Martin, and John Hay, waxed eloquent and emotional in front of the jury. Instead, Cooper lectured the jurors. "I have carefully avoided imputing any impropriety of intention to the President even in the very paper complained of — that the uniform tenor of my conduct and language has been to attribute honesty of motive even where I have strongly disapproved of the tendency of his measures."

By contrast, he implied, the prosecution was founded in the same atmosphere of overheated and partisan politics as had brought on the political crisis itself. "Gentlemen of the Jury, you, and all who hear me, well know that this country is divided, and almost equally divided, into two grand parties." The disagreements between them were substantial and relevant to the charges against him. Bearing in mind that everyone in the jury box had voted Federalist and was chosen by the federal marshal selected by Adams, Cooper probably realized that his line of defense, indeed any defense, was doomed. He was preaching in the wrong church. But this might be his last chance to give this sermon, and he was determined to finish it. The lines came straight out of his *Political Essays* — word for word. Apparently this was what he meant when he asked to return home to get his "papers" — he wanted his book draft.

Yet might he not try to persuade one or two members of the jury that he should not be convicted by appealing to their sense of fairness? His appeal rested on a theory of enlightened self-interest that had become current in late eighteenth-century English political and philosophical thought. People acted according to their perceived self-interest. "It is evident, Gentlemen of the Jury, that each [party] will view with a jealous eye the positions of the other, and that there cannot but be a bias among the partisans of the one side, against the principles and doctrines inculcated by the other." Such naked self-interest often led to disastrous results — a polity torn apart by unrelenting and unreasoning partisanship. The best results came from enlightened self-interest, as the Scottish political economist Adam Smith wrote in his *A Theory of Moral Sentiments* (1777), "regard to our own private happiness and interest appear to be laudable, but . . . self love . . . was vicious when it obstructed the public good." Cooper warned that self-interested partisanship was ripping the country apart. A guilty verdict would only widen that gulf.

> Although I have a right to presume something of political bias against my opinions, from the court who try me, to you who sit there as jurymen [I] am still satisfied you will feel, that you have some character to support and some character to lose; and whatever your opinions may be on the subjects alluded to in the indictment, you will reverence as you ought the sacred obligation of the oath you have taken.

Bias was natural, inevitable, but Cooper cast himself above such vices — and hoped the jury would as well.

Although Rawle was correct that governments at that time rarely allowed their critics freedom of expression, Cooper argued that the Sedition Act violated historical precedent. "Without impeaching the integrity of any person directly concerned in the progress of the present trial, I may fairly state, that under the sedition law, a defendant, such as I stand before you, is placed in a situation unknown in any other case." Cooper was referring once again to one of the most sacred maxims of the English common law: a man must not be a judge in his own cause. This time it was not just Adams's refusal to obey the subpoena that violated the maxim, but Chase and the court.

The maxim was first enunciated by Chief Justice Edward Coke in Dr. Bonham's Case (1610). Parliament had given to the Royal College of Physicians the right to judge whether any man might practice medicine. It was not a licensing statute, but a quasi-judicial one, for the punishment was a fine and imprisonment imposed by the Royal College. Coke struck down the statute because it allowed the guild to act as a judge in its own cause. Cooper applied the maxim to his own case. "Who nominates the judges who are to preside? The juries who are to judge of the evidence? the Marshal who has the summoning of the jury? The President." In a case involving the president's public reputation that very same individual had the power to name the judges and the jury.

Cooper's plea for fairness required certain concessions. "Gentlemen of the Jury, I acknowledge as freely as any of you can the necessary of a certain degree of confidence in the executive Government of the Country." But the world of politics had changed. With the arrival of a republican system of government, two national parties, and the First Amendment, "this confidence ought not be unlimited, and need not be paid up in advance, let it be earned before it be reposed; let it be claimed by the evidence of benefits conferred, of measures that compel approbation, of conduct irreproachable."

In a republican system, confidence resided in the sovereignty of the people, not the unlimited and unchecked sovereignty of an anointed ruler. That exercise of sovereignty was not limited to elections. For citizens could not cast an intelligent vote, indeed citizens could not be sure their vote would be accurately counted, without a free press. "It cannot be exacted by the guarded provisions of Sedition Laws, by attack on the Freedom of the Press, by prosecutions pains and penalties on those which boldly express the truth, or who may honestly and innocently err in their political sentiments."

Cooper's address had a modern ring to it, rooted as it was in basic concepts of democracy. But democracy was not what most of the framers had in mind when they wrote the Constitution, and democracy was certainly not favored in the ideology of the Federalists.

In the present state of affairs, the Press is open to those who will praise, while the threats of the Law hang over those who blame the conduct of the men in power. . . . Indiscriminate approbation of the measures of the executive, is not only unattached, but fostered and received with the utmost avidity. . . . While those who venture to express a sentiment of opposition must do it in fear and trembling, and run the hazard of being dragged like myself before the frowning tribunal, erected by the Sedition Law.

Cooper next tried to show the jury how biased Fenno's *Gazette of the United States* was, but Chase interrupted. "What is it that you say sir fell from [the lips of] the court? They have not yet decided what was or what was not proper evidence for you to adduce." Cooper had not submitted the copies of the newspaper to Chase and Peters. He could not read from them to the jury until they were admitted into evidence. Even if Cooper could show that Fenno used language far harsher and harder to prove true than Cooper's, such evidence was not material. It did not prove the truth of Cooper's comments, but only that the other side employed vituperation.

Fenno attacked those who criticized Adams and the Federalists. Because Cooper criticized those in power, he was liable to prosecution. Hirelings and scribblers paid by those in power to bash Cooper and other Republicans were safe so long as the Federalists controlled the courts, the Congress, and the executive branch, for the Republicans were not the government.

Cooper did not say anything more about who appointed the court or what the ulterior motives of the bench might be, but wary that Cooper would charge them with prejudice, the presiding judges relented. Peters opined, "I admit a great many things from Mr. Cooper who is without counsel, which I would not admit from others." Chase added, "You may read anything and everything you please." What Cooper did read was Fenno's attacks upon "the characters and conduct of the French rulers, and of the French nation." Again, this was irrelevant to his own case, merely showing that had Fenno lived in Paris instead of Philadelphia his head would have rested upon the base of the guillotine. In fact, the French Directory had no use for its own critics and suppressed them.

His own patience exhausted, Rawle interjected, "Does the court conceive this can be evidence?" Chase wryly opined, "Surely not; but let Mr. Cooper read what he pleases." One can see Chase waving his hand as if to dismiss what Cooper was saying at the same time as he allowed Cooper to speak. Once again insulted by Chase, this time Cooper conceded, "By no means: I shall not deliberately avail myself of what is not evidence, and perhaps this is not strictly so." As part of the ongoing newspaper debates, blasting Fenno was appropriate. As a matter of law in a trial, that is, as a defense to his own charges, it was not. "In a cause like this," Cooper hoped, "so completely political, I know the bias that may arise from these collateral suspicions and party imputations; and I wish if I can, to meet and to refute them as they arise." Plainly, his defense was on its last legs, and so was he. Time then for a last appeal to patriotism: "I am American enough to feel that both the belligerent powers have furnished us with a just cause for war, if common prudence had not forbidden resorting to it." The same common prudence should find him innocent of the charges.

Chase once again asked if Cooper wanted to call the witnesses. Cooper declined. It was getting late in the day; Cooper had spoken for hours. Chase wanted to finish. "Then if you do not mean to examine witnesses, the gentlemen who attend on this occasion need not be detained." Cooper conceded the point: "I shall not be able to go through with them." Chase could afford to be gracious. The die was almost cast. "Sir, the court do not want to press you; they will wait for an hour if you wish it to give you time to recruit your strength." Cooper was indeed exhausted. "I am much obliged to the court, and to the gentlemen who have attended, but I shall proceed and finish as soon as I can."

A weary Cooper closed.

> I think it impossible if you consider the paper [i.e., his broadside] all together that you can ascribe the publication of it to malice; it is on the face of it not voluntary but compelled. I have in the very outset of the paper spoken well of the President; I have been in the habit of thinking his intention right, and his public conduct wrong; and that this has been the general tenor of my language and behavior, I believe I can even now bring proof enough from among my friends and my neighbors.

Cooper offered to put two character witnesses on the stand. Chase reproved him. "This is not necessary. It is your conduct not your character that is in question. If this prosecution were for a crime against the United States, you might give evidence to your character and show that you have always been a good citizen, but this is an indictment for a libel against the President, where your general character is not in question." Actually, the Sedition Act punished crimes against the United States, a nice point on which Cooper was right and Chase wrong. But Cooper was done. "I shall fatigue the Jury no longer, . . . but rest my defense here."

Now came the closing scenes of the third act. Rawle had a case he could not lose, but he almost managed to do just that. For Cooper had argued that the issue was a dispute between himself and Adams, a private matter, and was not criminal at all. Rawle stumbled when he accepted Cooper's description of the event as a quarrel between two men.

> The defense you have just heard is one of the most extraordinary and unexampled I ever remember to have witnessed in a court of justice. It is no less than to call into decision whether Thomas Cooper, the defendant, or the President of the United States, to whom this country has thought proper to confide its most important interests is best qualified to judge whether the measures adopted by our governments are calculated to preserve the peace and promote the happiness of America.

Recognizing that he had one foot poised over a very slippery slope, he pulled himself back. "This, however, does not seem to me the real point which you are to try; and I shall therefore (under direction of the court) proceed to state what I conceive to be the question which you, Gentlemen of the Jury are now called upon to determine."

The parenthetical phrase in the account, "under direction of the court," was a telling proof of the cooperation of bench and prosecution; Cooper wanted his readers to know that the presiding judges had told Rawle how to present his case.

A chastened Rawle continued: "In the act which defines this offence, and points out the punishment, a liberality of defense is given, unknown I believe in any other Country where the party is tried for a libel on the Government." True enough—though at first the Federalists resisted adding this to the statute. "Here the defendant is allowed under the third section of that act to give evidence of the truth of the matters charged as a libel in the publication, and the Jury have a right to determine the Law and fact under the direction of the Court." Truth in America, unlike in England, was a defense.

The prosecution must also establish that the author's intent was malicious. "The defendant has undertaken to satisfy the mind of the Jury that in this publication he had no malicious intention against the President of the United States." But Rawle understood Cooper had written "in the clearest manner a settled design to persuade the public that the President of the United States is not fit for the high office he bears." Apparently, the test of maliciousness came not in the motive for writing the libel (the usual test of malice) but in the effect of the libel on the public mind. Rawle relied on Blackstone's reasoning; the crime was defined by its potential consequences.

But what were the actual consequences? No one could yet determine if, upon reading Cooper's blast, anyone contemplated sedition. What they might more likely contemplate was voting Republican. That was Cooper's desired effect, to sway the public mind against Adams. Was this kind of malice criminal in a republic? It was by Rawle's definition. Lest Cooper argue or the jury conclude that such publication was simply part of the Republican campaign to defeat Adams's reelection, Rawle continued that Cooper "cast an unmerited reflection on the general character and conduct of the President." But surely that was only grounds for a private suit Adams might file against Cooper, not for a prosecution for the crime of sedition.

Criminal law required that the defendant act with malice or at least indifference to the consequences of his actions. Rawle was arguing backward in time, that the consequent event proved the antecedent motive. Because (according to Rawle) Cooper's words had malicious effect, they must have had a malicious intent behind them. Rawle thus fell back upon the same sort of argument as Cooper's, albeit bent in the opposite direction. Cooper's words' likely consequences must be read as part of the politics of 1798. "Need I recall to your recollection the Summer of the year 1798 when in consequence of the disgraceful and insulting treatment and rejection of our envoys by the French Government, the Citizens of this Country from every part of the United States addressed the President approving his measures and pledging their support?" But Cooper, contrary to the great body of support for Adams, "proceeds to charge the President with unnecessary violence of official expression that might justly have provoked a war."

The problem with this argument was that Cooper was indicted for a November 1799 publication, a year after the XYZ affair and its domestic reception. Like the great orator Cicero in ancient Rome, who promised not to talk about something then spent an hour on it, Rawle promised, "It is not for me to dilate upon these topics, or on the depredations subsequently committed by that [French] Nation on the American Commerce, you all of you know, you all of you must have felt in some degree the consequence of her injustice."

Rawle was clearly pandering to the politics of the jury. He knew they were Federalists. It was only necessary to rouse their partisanship. His logic was flawed. His appeal to the jury's politics was flawless.

Chase applied the finishing touches to Rawle's summation in instructions to the jury. Judges' instructions to juries before they retire to consider their verdict educate the jurors on the law. Chase went beyond this to tell the jurors how to vote.

All governments which I have ever read or heard of punish libels against themselves. If a man attempts to destroy the confidence of the people in their officers, their supreme magistrate, and their legislature, he effectually saps the foundation of the government. A republican government can only be destroyed in two ways: the introduction of luxury, or the licentiousness of the press. This latter is the more slow, but most sure and certain, means of bringing about the destruction of the government.

In case the jury did not know exactly how to weigh the evidence, Chase made that plain too.

There is a little circumstance which the attorney-general [Rawle], in his observations to you, omitted to state, but which I think it right to recall to your recollection, as it appears with what design the traverser [Cooper] made this publication. In this allusion to Jonathan Robbins he expressly tells you this is "a case too little known, but of which the people ought to be fully apprised before the election, and they shall be." Here, then, the evident design of the traverser was, to arouse the people against the president so as to influence their minds against him on the next election. I think it right to explain this to you, because it proves, that the traverser was actuated by improper motives to make this charge against the president. It is a very heavy charge, and made with intent to bring the president into contempt and disrepute, and excite against him the hatred of the people of the United States.

The irony of Chase's virulent and unseemly partisanship on the bench was that he had in 1787 been an anti-federalist. The old saying that the convert is the most passionate and most orthodox believer was true in his case. He proved himself time and again an arch-Federalist in an office that was supposed to be above politics. Thus at this distance it seems almost embarrassing that Judge Peters added, after Chase addressed the jury, "I think we have nothing to do with parties; we are only to consider the subject before us."

But Chase's own slip of the tongue, his reference to the party contest over the forthcoming election, demonstrated what was most important to him. "Against him in the next election" was a reference to Adams's decision to run for reelection. Instead of "we have nothing to do with parties," Chase had proved the trial had everything to do with parties.

While historians still debate the appropriateness of Chase's conduct of this and the later seditious libel trials, it may be argued that he was simply following the letter of the law. It was not he who sought to turn the trial into a political carnival. It was not he who harangued bench and jury with political opinions. Chase's conduct of the trial was brusque, but he was on more than one occasion provoked. For the statute itself left Cooper little room to save himself, even if Chase had been more accommodating than he was. Chase was a partisan, and, in later trials of more obnoxious scribblers than the urbane and self-possessed Cooper, Chase would show more of his spleen. Here, one can say that the trial was, on balance, fair. It was the law that was censurable.

It took the jury a short time to reach its verdict. Cooper was convicted. Chase asked Cooper if he had the financial backing of a party, and, if so, the court would levy the maximum fine under the statute. Cooper denied that he wrote for a party, but conceded that some friends were ready to help him with the fine. It was said that Adams was tempted to pardon Cooper, but Cooper rejected the offer.

Cooper did not leave the trial record as the last word on the subject of freedom of the press. In his *Political Essays* (1800), published at the same time as the trial record, Cooper's copious praise of free inquiry enfolded freedom of the press within the larger freedom of thought. For "unlimited freedom of discussion" was essential "to the attainment of truth in fact, and truth in opinion. So, in our courts of justice, the utmost license of observation even on character is allowed, if it arise from any suggestion in the brief, or any fact in evidence." Cooper, sitting on the bench of the high court of truth, rendered an opinion contrary to Chase's. If one could pursue any line of argument in court, so long as it was relevant, in search of facts, why not in the public press? "All the evils objected to unlimited inquiry are partial and transient." Anticipating a famous U.S. Supreme Court dissent some 119 years in the future, Cooper called for a free marketplace of ideas.

Cooper left the Philadelphia jail on October 10, 1800, a free man. He was unchastened by the experience. During the course of his incarceration, the Federalist *Gazette of the United States* had made sport of him. Though he had put up the $2,000 bond for his future good behavior and could not attack the government, he had already fired off, in the words of his biographer Dumas Malone, a "fiery communication" to the *Gazette of the United States* attacking the paper. But coming home was sad, for his wife of twenty-one years, Alice Greenwood Cooper, had just succumbed to Philadelphia's endemic fevers. She had stayed in the city to be with him but did not live long enough to see him emerge from jail.

After his release, Cooper would go on to a career as a judge in Pennsylvania, and then as a professor of natural science at the University of Virginia (an appointment made before the school opened, but one he did not actually fill), Dickinson College, the University of Pennsylvania, and finally South Carolina College (later renamed the University of South Carolina). He was named president of the University of South Carolina in 1821 and served until 1833. His unconventional views of religion (he was a deist) became a cause of concern for conservative clergy, and he left his university post after some agitation against him. An early opponent of slavery, he changed his views dramatically when he went south. In Carolina he was a proslavery advocate. He was also a strong supporter of the doctrine of nullification, applying Jefferson's views in the Kentucky Resolves to South

Carolina's opposition to the Tariff of 1828. An intellectual gadfly to the end, Cooper died on May 11, 1839, after a lingering illness. Among the last pieces of his correspondence was a letter to newly elected President Martin Van Buren warning that the union could not endure if one section of the country proposed to dictate manners and morals to another section.

But Cooper's trial and conviction did not close the story of the Sedition Act. The consequences of the act, including the arguments made for and against it, would soon move in unexpected and remarkable directions, posing an even greater threat to the nation than Cooper prophesied at his trial.

The Unforeseen (and Unintended) Consequences of the Sedition Act Crisis

Irony is a staple of history. Our plans do not work out as we wish; our actions have unexpected consequences; our ideas change their implications and applications in unforeseen ways. Irony was everywhere in the unforeseen consequences of the Sedition Act crisis.

It was ironic that the Republican press stepped up its attacks on Adams's preparations for war at the same time as Adams's eleventh-hour diplomacy averted an open breach with France. He reached out once more to the French government, and this time the French were more accommodating. To Hamilton's consternation, the drum beat for a patriotic war ceased. So furious was Hamilton at Adams for this and the pardon of Fries that Hamilton published his own scathingly critical essay on all Adams's failures. Hamilton was not indicted for violating the Sedition Act, though much of what he said was far more vituperative and condemnatory than anything the Republicans wrote.

One reason that Hamilton may have been furious at Adams was that, for Hamilton at least, the justification for all of the four Federalist enactments was the coming war with France. In fact, legal historian John Witt has persuasively argued that Hamilton based his support for the acts on the international law of war, to wit, that in time of war a sovereign government could order alien enemies to depart immediately and could silence its critics. The Federalists need not rely on the thin reed of the elastic clause. The far stronger weaving of the laws of war and peace explicitly conferred this authority upon the commander in chief — John Adams. But Adams had, in effect, dispensed with the powers that Hamilton's argument had conferred. Seen in another light, then, what was a vituperative political combat was also a dispute over a legal issue, by two superbly able lawyers, Hamilton and Adams, in the court of public opinion.

But the sedition trials went on apace. Under the act, twenty-five

Republican editors, political writers, and a congressman were arrested, and seventeen indictments, fourteen of which came under the Sedition Act, were handed down by grand juries (the grand juries did not find true bills in the other cases). Eleven of the indictments actually were tried, and all of the defendants were convicted.

With Lyon's travail and Cooper's trial before them, Republican writers such as the Scottish immigrant James Callender ran for cover. Though Callender thought himself safe in Virginia, federal attorney Thomas Nelson summoned a grand jury there to indict Callender for writing in his *The Prospect before Us* that the "reign of Mr. Adams has hitherto been one continued tempest of malignant passions. As president, he has never opened his lips, or lifted his pen, without threatening and scolding. The grand object of his administration has been to exasperate the rage of contending parties, to calumniate and destroy every man who differs from his opinions." The handpicked grand jury found a true bill on May 24, 1800; trial began on June 3; and after the jury found Callender guilty, on June 4 Justice Chase sentenced Callender to nine months in jail.

In fact, Callender's *The Prospect before Us* had so infuriated Justice Chase that he insisted the jury find Callender guilty. If, and only if, Callender could show that every word he wrote was true, could they acquit him. Once again this was the English civil libel doctrine of proof "to the marrow," placing on the defendant the burden of proving that every word was fact. The doctrine advanced in Cooper's case became the rule in Callender's. The Richmond, Virginia, jury, chastened by the bench (Chase abandoning any pose of objectivity to reinforce Nelson's argument with his own instructions), found him guilty.

In the course of their defense of Callender, his attorneys George Hay and Philip Nicholas (both of whom would gain office under Jefferson), tried to argue that Callender should be allowed to present evidence that his words were true. Chase demanded to see the evidence, in writing, before he would allow it in open court. When he saw it, he ruled that it was too prejudicial — that is, that it would "deceive and mislead the jury." When a third counsel, William Wirt, a leading Richmond lawyer, asked permission to address the jury on the constitutionality of the Sedition Law, Chase once again stepped in and squelched counsel.

All three lawyers argued for the Virginia rule, that Chase should be bound by state procedure, and that procedure allowed them to present evidence of truth. He sneered that they argued non sequitur, a term of logic he misused. In the end, they left the court and their client to the not-so-tender mercies of the bench. Chase's conduct of the trial would come back to haunt him, becoming one of the articles on which the House of Representatives impeached him and the Senate tried him in 1805.

With Benjamin Bache dead, William Duane continued publication of the *Aurora*. He lacked Bache's gift for personal vituperation, but he shared Bache's politics. He so infuriated the Federalists in the Senate (accusing them of a tyrannous conspiracy) that they ordered him to appear before the Senate to explain himself. He retained counsel — Alexander Dallas and Thomas Cooper — but was informed he had no right to counsel there. Duane was a no-show, as were his attorneys, who declined to serve, and in fact Duane surfaced only after Congress had gone into recess, and the summons lapsed. It was all, in the words of historians Stanley Elkins and Eric McKitrick, "damp fireworks." But the Sedition Act's fuse was still lit.

On October 17, 1800, a federal grand jury handed down an indictment against Duane for seditious libel under the 1798 law. Dallas again stepped forward for the defense. Federal prosecutor Jared Ingersoll, like Rawle and unlike Nelson, was of two minds about the prosecution. He allowed a commission to take evidence that Duane needed to prove the truth of his printed words. By the time he came to trial, in May 1801, Jefferson was president and offered his aid to Duane, limited by his recognition that the judiciary and the executive were separate branches of government. In the end, a new grand jury, summoned by Jefferson's choice of marshal, found no grounds for the indictment.

As the seditious libel trials were tied to the election of 1800, so was the fate of the Sedition Act. The Republican press had survived the Federalist assault. Duane's *Aurora* was not silenced. The *Aurora* of October 14, 1800, included an editorial entitled "Citizens of Philadelphia Take Your Choice," and readers had no doubt where Duane stood. "Things as they have been" included "the principles and patriots of the Revolution condemned and stigmatized; the nation in arms without a foe and the nation divided without cause; a reign of terror created by false alarms, to promote domestic feuds and foreign war . . .

a sedition law to protect corrupt magistrates and public defaulters."
By contrast, "things as they will be" presumably after a Republican
victory, "the nation at peace with the world, and united in itself . . .
allaying the fever of domestic feuds and subduing opposition by the
force of reason and rectitude; good government without the aid of
priestcraft, or religious politics, and justice administered without
political intolerance."

It was ironic that in the election, with fears of war abated, the
Republicans were able to turn the Alien and Sedition Acts to advantage. The focal point of this electoral effort was a smear campaign
against Adams in Republican newspapers and pamphlets. In vain federal prosecutors had tried to muzzle scandalmongers such as Callender. On October 6, 1799, Jefferson privately wrote to Callender "such
papers cannot fail to have the best effect." They did. The Republicans
defeated the Federalists in the presidential and most of the congressional contests (though a more unified Federalist Party might have
retained the presidency).

The U.S. Supreme Court never heard an appeal of the Sedition Act
prosecutions. No appeal was filed, at least. What might the Court have
decided? In the trial of Lyon, Justice William Paterson told the jury
that it must "treat the law as valid," until such time as the High Court
reviewed it. He did write a tentative opinion, never published or even
circulated, that anticipated *Marbury v. Madison*'s claim of judicial
review of acts of Congress. He also opined that the act was fully within
the constitutional capacities of Congress. Both Justices William Cushing and Samuel Chase, while presiding at circuit court sessions, warned
juries about the licentiousness that libelous political speech promoted.
U.S. Supreme Court Chief Justice Oliver Ellsworth, writing privately
to Pickering on December 12, 1798, agreed that the act "does not create an offense, but rather, by permitting the truth of the libel to be
given in justification, causes that, in some cases, not to be an offense
which was one before." There can be little doubt that the High Court,
Federalist to a man, would have sustained the Sedition Act.

By contrast, arguably the foremost legal scholar of the day, St.
George Tucker of Virginia, opined that the Blackstonean view of seditious libel did not belong in American jurisprudence. Tucker shunned
the political arena. His scholarship and professionalism in law elevated
him above the clamor of parties — a rare feat in these partisan days.

Tucker's 1802–1803 commentaries on Blackstone's *Commentaries* included notes and appendixes comparing English common law to the developing law of the independent state of Virginia. It was an indispensable aid to Virginia lawyers and judges, including those who might hear seditious libel cases under state law. In some states, prosecutors still cited Blackstone as good authority—the greater the truth, the more dangerous the publication of it. Tucker disagreed. The freedom of the press was "absolute" save for suits for defamation of character by private individuals against one another. Tucker continued that

if the legislature should pass a law dangerous to the liberties of the people, the judiciary are bound to pronounce, not only whether the party accused hath been guilty of any violation of it, but whether such a law be permitted by the constitution. . . . The judiciary, therefore, is that department of the government to whom the protection of the rights of the individual is by the constitution especially confided, interposing its shield between him and the sword of usurped authority, the darts of oppression, and the shafts of faction and violence.

What faction, violence, and usurped authority could Tucker mean? The Federalist majority that passed the Sedition Act and the prosecutors who used it to muzzle the Republican press. But the federal courts did protect the liberties of the people during the Sedition Act crisis. "On the trial of Mr. Thomas Cooper, in the federal circuit court in Pennsylvania, for a libel against the president of the United States, under the sedition law. . . . The case was certainly delicate, and might have been perplexing." And that hint was as far as Tucker would go.

Tucker's views to the contrary notwithstanding, in future years no federal court would declare a sedition act unconstitutional, not the act of 1798, nor its successors in 1918 or 1940. The power of Congress to define and punish sedition has been on occasion nibbled away at by the High Court, but never wholly denied to the legislative branch.

The story of the Sedition Act prosecutions and of the Federalist attempt to use the law to muzzle Republican opposition should have ended in 1801. After all, in 1801 Jefferson entered the White House for the first of his two terms. Jefferson's first inaugural address promised that erroneous political opinions would not be suppressed; "let them stand undisturbed as monuments of the safety with which error of opinion may be tolerated, where reason is left free to combat it." Jefferson allowed the Sedition Act to lapse, though various states continued to prosecute unpopular political speech under state law, including courts in Jefferson's own state. The First Amendment did not touch these cases, though guarantees of freedom of the press in state constitutions did apply. Legal scholar Akhil Reed Amar and others have argued that the "revolution of 1800" that brought Jefferson and his party to power effectively repealed the Sedition Act and privileged freedom of the press.

But privately Jefferson fumed about the "false facts" that Federalists had spewed and would continue to spew against him and his administration. He had told Levi Lincoln, the attorney general, on March 24, 1802, "I would wish much to see the experiment tried of getting along without public prosecutions for libels. I believe we can do it." A year later, the experiment was over. He informed Thomas McKean, on February 19, 1803, it was time for the "Tory presses'" lying "to be deprived of all credit" by prosecution. As he wrote to Abigail Adams, on September 11, 1804, the "overwhelming torrent of slander, which is confounding all vice and virtue, all truth and falsehood" could still be stemmed by state enactments. The shoe, it appears, was now on the other foot and pinched Jefferson as badly as it had Adams.

The Jeffersonian Republicans next turned their attention to the Federalist judiciary. In the final days of his presidency, John Adams had signed the Judiciary Act of 1801 into law. It created an intermediate tier of circuit courts of appeal between the district trial courts and the High Court, relieving the Supreme Court justices of the burden of riding circuit and presiding over trials. This made sense, for the justices under the existing system had to hear appeals from the rulings they themselves made during the trials. But to the benches of these new appeals courts, Adams appointed only Federalists, a step that looked like a way to ensure Federalist control of one branch of the Federal government.

When they came to power, the Jeffersonians not only repealed the Judiciary Act of 1801, denying to the Federalists these new judgeships, but the Republican majority in the Congress then passed another Judiciary Act, in April, refashioning the federal circuit courts into six cir-

cuits (leaving in place a D.C. circuit court) and, in June of 1802, post-
poning the next session of the Supreme Court until February of 1803.
Perhaps by then the Federalists on the High Court would retire (or
die) and their seats could be filled with good Republicans. When that
did not occur, the plan then called for a series of impeachments and
trials of the judges who presided at the Sedition Act trials. First was
New Hampshire district court Judge John Pickering. His case was
easy. He was an alcoholic whose psychotic episodes left him unfit him
for the post. He was convicted by the Senate and removed from office.
Next came Justice Chase. Chase had harassed defense counsel and
harangued grand juries during the sedition trials, spewing his own
partisanship about the courtroom. But the managers of his impeachment could not gain the two-thirds vote necessary to convict him in
the Senate on any of the impeachment counts. He died in 1811 while
still a member of the High Court.

Jefferson left office in 1809, as war with Britain loomed. His actions
as president, particularly in the purchase of the Louisiana Territory
and the enforcement of the Embargo Act of 1808, showed a political
skill that Adams lacked and a willingness to use executive authority
that Adams never contemplated. For his performance in this role, Jefferson can be cited as the first of the modern chief executives. He
retired to Monticello, rarely traveled, and enjoyed the comforts of
family and the services of more than 200 slaves until his death in 1826.
His legacy as a defender of the freedom of the press was a mixed one —
strong when he was in the minority, weaker when he was in a position
to use law to suppress dissent.

Obviously, the vituperation of the first great national parties had
not lessened during Jefferson's tenure. The project of wholesale prosecutions of dissenting political figures by a party in control of the
executive and both houses of Congress fizzled, but the political precedent and its legal consequences that the Sedition Act of 1798 created
did not disappear from disuse. Instead, in times of crisis the opposing
doctrines that the Federalists and their Republican opponents of 1798
had promulgated took on new forms, sometimes more ominous ones
than the originals.

By the time that they had served the nation as its president, both
Madison and Jefferson realized the dangerous implications of inter-

position and nullification and agreed that both were impossible within the frame of the Constitution. A state could not constitutionally interpose itself between its citizens and the federal government, for every citizen of a state was also a citizen of the federal government. But ideas have a way of moving beyond the intentions of their framers, and by 1828, nullification had gained a life of its own under the nurturing care of John C. Calhoun of South Carolina.

That Calhoun became the advocate of nullification was itself ironic. He was educated at Yale College and then prepared himself for a career as a lawyer at Tapping Reeve's school in Connecticut. Returning to South Carolina, he practiced off and on in his native state, but his major occupation was politics. He was an early advocate of universal male suffrage, and when he entered national politics in 1810, he strongly supported a protective tariff, internal improvements, and expenditures for national defense. What might have become a career of progressive and reforming nationalism sharply shifted as his prospects for the highest office dimmed.

By the middle of the 1820s, his commitment to the nation had been replaced by an equally fervent sectionalism. The motive may have been a foreshortening of his ambition to be president, but his views closely paralleled those of other leading South Carolinians. Increasingly, they felt isolated from the major trends of national politics and economic development. The protective tariffs of the 1820s, culminating in the 1828 "tariff of abominations," favored the textile-producing states of the Northeast over the cotton-exporting states of the Southeast. In 1827, Calhoun wrote despairingly, "It seems to me, that the despotism founded on combined geographical interest [in Congress] admits of but one effectual remedy, a veto . . . on the part of the states."

In his secretly authored "Exposition" of 1828 for the South Carolina legislature, Calhoun proposed that the Constitution was not an organic and permanent form of government, but a contract or compact among sovereign states, and states could judge for themselves whether any act of the federal government applied to that state's citizens. It was a well-argued legal brief for nullification, the doctrine borrowed from Jefferson's Kentucky Resolves and put to work to explain why the South Carolina legislature could pass a law preventing the collection of the tariff in South Carolina ports. South Carolina lawmakers would thereby decide for themselves the constitutionality of a federal law. This flew in the face of the Constitution itself, Article I explicitly delegating to Congress the authority to lay tariffs and Article VI stating that the Constitution and the laws made under it were the supreme law of the land.

To support his contrary view of congressional power, Calhoun proposed that the Constitution was nothing more than a contract among sovereign states, the so-called compact theory. Under it, nullification, and even secession, were legitimate. The opening sentences of the "Exposition" sounded like the Virginia and Kentucky Resolutions; then Calhoun's language became more strident. The argument for strict construction of the Constitution, first proposed by the Jeffersonians, might have ruled out a Sedition Act. But Article I of the Constitution explicitly gave to Congress the sole authority to lay tariffs. Calhoun had to navigate around this apparently open-ended grant. He did so with verve – "The Constitution grants to Congress the power of imposing a duty on imports for revenue; which power is abused by being converted into an instrument for rearing up the industry of one section of the country on the ruins of another. The violation then consists in using a power, granted for one object, to advance another, and that by the sacrifice of the original object."

Calhoun regretted the sectional and self-interested character of the rest of the "Exposition," but he insisted that the Constitution was a compact, a contract like any other, among the various states, and the contracting parties might negate those laws violating their vital interests. After all, the federal government was the creature of the states, not the reverse. The only way to prevent the minority from being oppressed by the majority, in this case South Carolina by the majority of the other states, was to give to each state a veto power over federal law. Then the "concurrent majority" would not be oppressed.

The protest against the federal Sedition Act of 1798 had thus born this third, still unripe, fruit.

With these views the committee are solemnly of impression if the system be persevered in, after due forbearance on the part of the State, that it will be her sacred duty to interpose her veto; a duty to herself, to the Union, to present, and to future generations, and to the cause of liberty over the world, to arrest the progress of a power, which, if not arrested, must in its consequences, corrupt the public morals, and destroy the liberty of the country.

Had Jefferson said anything different in 1798?

The South was the region where the Jefferson-Madison ideal of freedom of political expression took strongest root, but in the antebellum era certain kinds of publications were deemed so potentially inflammatory that local authorities, on their own initiative, banned their distribution. As the abolitionists of the North began to publish accounts of the evils of slavery, southern political leaders grew more concerned about the impact of abolitionism on the South's "peculiar institution." Abolitionist tracts were burned and abolitionist speakers driven to cover.

Led by its southern members, in 1836, the House of Representatives and the Senate voted a "gag rule," denying to congressmen the right to read aloud, when Congress was in session, abolition petitions. According to the advocates of the gag rule, it did not abridge the right to petition, nor was the freedom of speech and press of the representatives chilled. They just could not read the petitions aloud in Congress. When former President John Quincy Adams, now a representative from Massachusetts, tried to read a petition to free slaves in the District of Columbia, southern congressmen demanded that he be censured. On February 6, 1837, Calhoun explained why a gag rule was essential.

We are now told that the most effectual mode of arresting the progress of abolition is, to reason it down; and with this view it is urged that the [antislavery] petitions ought to be referred to a committee. That is the very ground which was taken at the last session in the [House of Representatives] but instead of arresting its progress it has since advanced more rapidly than ever. . . . As widely as this incendiary spirit has spread, it has not yet infected this body, or the great mass of the intelligent and business portion of the North; but unless it be speedily stopped, it will spread and work upwards till it brings the two great sections of the Union into deadly conflict.

In effect, the petitions had a dangerous tendency of causing further controversy, and, worse, of spreading the doctrines of antislavery. That was the Blackstonean justification for seditious libel law. Calhoun did not fully credit the "Congress shall make no law" formula, for he knew that free speech on the subject of slavery was already dead in the South.

In the shadows of the doctrine of nullification and the implementation of the gag rule lay an even more ominous notion: secession. The real concern of South Carolina's political leadership was what Congress might do with slavery. Slaves were a majority of the state's population, by far the greatest source of wealth in the state, and their labor was vital to the rice and cotton crops that sustained the state's economy. If a majority of northern and eastern interests in Congress could pass a tariff that ignored South Carolina's protests, might Congress also constrain slavery (for example, by barring the internal slave trade), to the state's detriment? By 1850, with Congress reeling from a decade of bitter debates over slavery, the annexation of Texas, the Mexican-American War, and the admission of California as a free state, Calhoun warned that southern states might take nullification a step farther, to secede from the Union. On March 4, 1850, he lay on a sedan chair in the senate chamber, dying, as a colleague read these words to the members:

> Unless something decisive is done, I again ask, What is to stop this agitation before the great and final object at which it aims — the abolition of slavery in the States — is consummated? Is it, then, not certain that if something is not done to arrest it, the South will be forced to choose between abolition and secession? Indeed, as events are now moving, it will not require the South to secede in order to dissolve the Union. Agitation will of itself effect it, of which its past history furnishes abundant proof. . . . Disunion must be the work of time. It is only through a long process, and successively, that the cords can be snapped until the whole fabric falls asunder. Already the agitation of the slavery question has snapped some of the most important, and has greatly weakened all the others. . . . If the agitation goes on, the same force, acting with increased intensity, as has been shown, will finally snap every cord, when nothing will be left to hold the States together except force.

With the election of Abraham Lincoln to the presidency in 1860, South Carolina seceded from the Union. In yet another ironic twist to the story, secession of the southern states spurred the federal government to revisit the Sedition Act formula. In the Virginia secession convention, for example, secessionists "based their arguments on the Virginia and Kentucky resolutions of 1798." Even in the North on the eve of battle some Democrats warned that "there exists in the so-called free North today a petty tyranny of opinion and expression, which outrivals in its malignant hatred of free institutions and popular government, the worst despotism of ancient or modern times."

During the Civil War, Lincoln had little hesitation about curbing the speech of pro-Confederate and antiwar politicians. In effect, he adopted the Federalist program on speech — speech that was too freely pro-Confederacy had the dangerous consequence of undermining the Union war effort. He employed military courts to suppress speech that would sabotage the war effort. The goal — the survival of the Union — trumped any qualms about free speech. Politics played a vital part in these affairs. Lincoln feared that pro-southern speakers might cause the Republican Party to lose control of Congress and even defeat him in the 1864 presidential election.

Thus, when Indiana Democrat Clement Vallandigham attacked Lincoln's war policies as "wicked, cruel, and unnecessary" at a mass political gathering during the Ohio Democratic state convention, Lincoln ordered his arrest and trial before a military tribunal for "publicly expressing . . . sympathy for those in arms against the government of the United States, and declaring disloyal sentiments and opinions with the object and purpose of weakening the power of the government in its efforts to suppress an unlawful rebellion." The danger was that his listeners might act upon their disloyalty. He was convicted, and his appeal to the regular federal courts was denied. Lincoln ordered Vallandigham expelled from the United States, and the president remained unmoved on the issue, despite a torrent of protest in Democratic newspapers. He did shift his ground, however, when he explained to his critics that Vallandigham was punished not for expressing his opinions, but for hindering the recruitment effort. Running for governor of Ohio from a hotel room in Windsor, Ontario (the Democrats in Ohio had nominated him), Vallandigham called himself a champion of freedom of the press.

Vallandigham's conduct would have been criminal under the Sedition Act of 1798. So, too, it would have violated the Espionage Act of 1917 and the Sedition Act of 1918 that Congress passed and the presi-

{ *Chapter 6* }

dent signed into law. In time of perceived national emergency and threatened party strife, the precedent of 1798 came alive. The World War I acts originally allowed the president sole and complete discretion in determining who had violated the act and who might be expelled from the country or jailed for violating the act, but cooler heads in the Congress prevailed and the final drafts provided for trial at law. The provisions were similar to those of the Sedition Act of 1798:

Whoever when the United States is at war, shall willfully utter, print, write or publish any disloyal, profane, scurrilous, or abusive language about the form of government of the United States or the Constitution of the United States, or the military or naval forces of the United States, or the flag of the United States, or the uniform of the Army or Navy of the United States into contempt, scorn, contumely, or disrepute, or shall willfully utter, print, write, or publish any language intended to incite, provoke, or encourage resistance to the United States . . . shall be punished by a fine of not more than $10,000 or the imprisonment for not more than twenty years, or both.

There were dissenting voices, just as in 1798. Among these were Socialist leader Eugene V. Debs. Socialism, the cause of the oppressed masses, had "given me my ideas and ideals, my principles and convictions." For opposing the war effort, Debs was convicted under the statute. Supreme Court Justice Oliver Wendell Holmes Jr. of Massachusetts initially supported the prosecutions under the Sedition Act — he wrote the opinion upholding Debs's conviction — but by 1919, he had second thoughts. In *Abrams v. U.S.*, Holmes expressed those thoughts in language that would become landmarks in our constitutional landscape. The five defendants in *Abrams v. U.S.*, all young anarchists born in Russia, dropped leaflets in English and Yiddish from a Lower East Side, Manhattan, window criticizing President Wilson's silence about the allies' opposition to the Bolshevik Revolution. There was no clear and present danger to the country, but the majority, with Justice Clarke citing the three earlier Holmes opinions, found that the leaflets violated the Espionage Acts. The Court's majority rejected the defendants' contention that their only intent was to prevent injury to the Russian cause, holding that men had to be held to have intended, and had to be accountable for, the effects that their acts were likely to produce.

Holmes's dissent has become famous:

> But as against dangers peculiar to war, as against others, the principle of the right to free speech is always the same. It is only the present danger of immediate evil or an intent to bring it about that warrants Congress in setting a limit to the expression of opinion where private rights are not concerned. Congress certainly cannot forbid all effort to change the mind of the country. . . . Persecution for the expression of opinions seems to me perfectly logical. If you have no doubt of your premises or your power and want a certain result with all your heart you naturally express your wishes in law and sweep away all opposition. . . . But when men have realized that time has upset many fighting faiths, they may come to believe even more than they believe the very foundations of their own conduct that the ultimate good desired is better reached by free trade in ideas — that the best test of truth is the power of the thought to get itself accepted in the competition of the market, and that truth is the only ground upon which their wishes safely can be carried out. That at any rate is the theory of our Constitution. It is an experiment, as all life is an experiment. Every year if not every day we have to wager our salvation upon some prophecy based upon imperfect knowledge. While that experiment is part of our system I think that we should be eternally vigilant against attempts to check the expression of opinions that we loathe and believe to be fraught with death, unless they so imminently threaten immediate interference with the lawful and pressing purposes of the law that an immediate check is required to save the country.

Holmes had more to say about the ancestor of the World War I sedition acts:

> I wholly disagree with the argument of the Government that the First Amendment left the common law as to seditious libel in force. History seems to me against the notion. I had conceived that the

United States through many years had shown its repentance for the Sedition Act of 1798, by repaying fines that it imposed. Only the emergency that makes it immediately dangerous to leave the correction of evil counsels to time warrants making any exception to the sweeping command, "Congress shall make no law . . . abridging the freedom of speech." Of course I am speaking only of expressions of opinion and exhortations, which were all that were uttered here, but I regret that I cannot put into more impressive words my belief that in their conviction upon this indictment the defendants were deprived of their rights under the Constitution of the United States.

Under the terms of the Alien Registration Act (so-called Smith Act) of 1940, prosecutions for sedition reappeared. The act provided that it was a felony to "knowingly or willfully advocate, abet, advise, or teach the duty, necessity, desirability, or propriety of overthrowing the Government of the United States or of any State by force or violence, or for anyone to organize any association which teaches, advises, or encourages such an overthrow, or for anyone to become a member of, or to affiliate with, any such association." Aliens, as in 1798, were the special target of the act. They were to register with the federal government or face the danger of deportation. The act was used against the Socialist Workers Party, communists who opposed American entry into World War II (before the Nazis invaded the Soviet Union), a group of Nazi sympathizers in 1944, and the Communist Party of the United States in 1949.

The act is still on the books, but its prohibition of publication, distribution, and study of allegedly subversive words has been severely curtailed by the U.S. Supreme Court. This portion of the arguments that Jefferson and Madison made in favor of freedom of the press over two hundred years ago has won the day, at least for now. As the Supreme Court finally decreed, in *Yates v. United States* (1957), a lecture, a meeting, a conversation, or a publication teaching an abstract doctrine that might, if effected, lead to the violent overthrow of the government was not the same as speech that directly and immediately incited illegal actions. "It is argued that advocacy of forcible overthrow as mere abstract doctrine is within the free speech protection of the First Amendment; that the Smith Act, consistently with that constitutional provision, must be taken as proscribing only the sort of advocacy which incites to illegal action." The "paper walls" of the First Amendment stood. "We are thus faced with the question whether the Smith Act prohibits advocacy and teaching of forcible overthrow as an abstract principle, divorced from any effort to instigate action to that end, so long as such advocacy or teaching is engaged in with evil intent. We hold that it does not."

One may, with such distinguished company as the First Amendment scholar Anthony Lewis, see the long line of sedition acts, beginning with 1798, as a landmark of freedom because "it made a number of Americans appreciate the importance of free speech and freedom of the press." But as Lewis continued, the act established another, more sinister precedent. It proved that fear of repression could chill freedom of speech — the very prior censorship that the act's advocates disclaimed. The severe penalties of the 1798 act were repeated in the Espionage Act of 1917 and the Smith Act, penalties far out of proportion to the danger of mere words.

The temptation to quash public debate in the name of national unity in time of national emergency will never disappear. As distinguished constitutional historian Stanley Kutler reminds us, "the reality is that power holders do sometimes subvert the law and cynically manipulate it to their own ends." Indeed, it is that simple dismaying fact that makes freedom of the press so vital to all our other freedoms. For it was a free press that challenged power even as those in power attempted to muzzle the press. The debate over freedom of speech and the press, begun in the first years of the new nation, will continue so long as those in power decide that patriotic spirit in times of national peril is more important than the limitations on government the framers imposed.

It is the nature of irony in history that there is no final irony. The twisted reading of protests arising out of the Sedition Act continues to bedevil American politics. By the end of the 1950s, as the debate over the suppression of antigovernment prints quieted, interposition and nullification blossomed once again. "Massive resistance" in the Deep South to Civil Rights law spawned new versions of older states' rights manifestos. Spouting these theories, governors and legislatures interposed themselves between federal desegregation mandates and the states' white citizens. They looked to history for inspiration and example. The enemy was once again the federal government. As a bloc of southern members of Congress announced in 1956, "We regard the decisions of the Supreme Court in the school cases as a clear abuse of judicial power. It climaxes a trend in the Federal Judiciary undertaking to legislate, in derogation of the authority of Congress, and to encroach upon the reserved rights of the States and the people." Through the 1960s, segregationist southern politicians practiced a hit-and-run form of interposition, dragging their feet, railing at a second federal invasion of the South, and displaying bad faith when ordered to comply with the law.

Conclusion

The Paper Barriers

Thomas Cooper was not a major political figure in the partisan battles of the 1790s. That he, and his broadside, could be singled out for prosecution reminded the Republicans that all of them were vulnerable. The passage of and the trials following the Sedition Act of 1798 were the first great test of the speech and press provisions of the First Amendment. But the notion that law is made through a series of tests implies that the passing of time, like the passing of tests, is a simple upward progress. Instead, if the later course of free speech law is any example, the course of the law in our history is not a steady upward progress but a twisting and sometimes unpredictable spiral. So too was the course of the arguments made against the law — not only for freedom of the press, but for the ability of states to interpose themselves between their citizens and the national government.

The Sedition Act and the protests against it took on lives of their own. They mutated as different generations used and reused the words and ideas. With each passage of arms, freedom of speech and press grew more robust and government more intrusive. As if they were somehow linked, a kind of thesis and antithesis, opposition to government and increasing government power over everyday life fueled one another, taking on new forms as civil rights and liberties moved to the center of American jurisprudence.

Free speech became more inclusive not because the law worked its way toward greater liberality, but because the nation became more inclusive and democratic. The law mirrored that growth. As more and more people found their voices, the law accommodated a greater variety of public speech. The Coopers and all the others who risked prosecution to speak may not have had pure motives nor sought public martyrdom. They may not have been courageous people, though their actions were courageous. Democracy, to succeed, does not need martyrs or heroes. Instead, the Coopers and all who followed were engaging in a basic democratic exercise. They were voicing their opinion in opposition to power. As Justice Louis Brandeis wrote, in *Whitney v. California* (1926):

> Those who won our independence believed that the final end of the State was to make men free to develop their faculties; and that in its government the deliberative forces should prevail over the arbitrary. . . . They believed that freedom to think as you will and to speak as you think are means indispensable to the discovery and spread of political truth; that without free speech and assembly discussion would be futile; that with them, discussion affords ordinarily adequate protection against the dissemination of noxious doctrine; that the greatest menace to freedom is an inert people; that public discussion is a political duty; and that this should be a fundamental principle of the American government.

Over time, the protection that law afforded the reputation — the private lives and public esteem — of public figures began to erode. By the end of the 1960s, the U.S. Supreme Court required only that the newspaper publishing a criticism or observation of a public figure not wantonly or recklessly disregard the truth. Fame and power brought with them publicity both good and bad. When the Court struck down an Alabama libel award against the *New York Times*, the decision was unanimous. The commissioners of Birmingham could not claim protection against an NAACP advertisement claiming they misused their powers. Justice William Brennan wrote for the Court:

> Although the Sedition Act was never tested in this Court, the attack upon its validity has carried the day in the court of history. . . . The constitutional guarantees require, we think, a federal rule that prohibits a public official from recovering damages for a defamatory falsehood relating to his official conduct unless he proves that the statement was made with "actual malice" — that is, with knowledge that it was false or with reckless disregard of whether it was false or not.

But the verdict of history is not quite as certain or as secure as Justice Brennan thought in 1964. Whenever those in power decide that critics must be silenced, some version of the Sedition Act has reappeared. If the "paper walls," in Madison's words, against such official acts do not protect the dissenter and the protestor, democracy itself is imperiled. One can see this in other countries, where criticism of the government or unpatriotic statements of any kind are serious offenses subject to criminal prosecution. In such countries, democracy is either frail or nonexistent. A robust free press is not a guarantee that suppression is impossible, but it is a proof that democracy is alive and well.

The claim of state politicians (or federal officials for that matter) that the state government is some sort of shield protecting the people of the state against the federal government has its own troubled but illuminating history. Applied to freedom of the press in the 1790s, the shield of states' rights seemed to protect basic freedoms; applied to slavery in the antebellum period, the doctrine denied freedom for bondmen and -women; applied to civil rights, the notion undergirded white dominion over black; renamed "new judicial federalism" in the 1970s, it found in state constitutions greater protection for civil rights than the Court found in the federal Constitution. Like freedom of the press, states' rights are a legal chameleon, able to take on new colors as its background changes.

Still, history is full of lessons for those who want to learn. The application of the lessons is not always easy, but always worth the effort. The lesson of the story of the Sedition Act of 1798 is that the liberties we cherish are not always proof against power and partisanship. We have to guard them zealously. This is not to condone or protect totally irresponsible journalism, particularly when the boundaries of opinion have extended to the utmost reaches of the blogosphere. Private suits for defamation cannot curb the excesses of Web-based paparazzi. Asking political figures to "lump it" when their private lives become public melodramas is not entirely fair. It is not easy to strike a balance between privacy and right to know. But whatever stand one takes on this issue, officially imposed curbs on political opinion in the press, particularly when that opinion is critical of those in power, is a step on the way to the loss of all our liberties.

So, too, the lessons of the Kentucky and Virginia Resolves are hard won and never secure. The real lesson is that law can confront power with powerful arguments, but those arguments can all too easily be detached from the context in which they are made and put to other uses. The argument itself should never be offered apart from its circumstances. That lesson must be taught to each generation of Americans, especially those who apply and interpret our laws. How easy it has become for lawyers or law professors to ignore those lessons when they serve in or advise government.

CHRONOLOGY

1606	Seditious libel defined as crime in England to include writings published that bring into contempt the Crown, the government, or any of its principals, as distinguished from sedition—acts or conspiring to act against the government—and libel, the civil tort of publishing falsehoods with the intention to defame a private individual.
1640s	Some advocates of freedom of discourse in England introduce the term "freedom of speech."
August 4, 1735	Andrew Hamilton defends John Peter Zenger on the charge of common law seditious libel of governor William Cosby.
1759	Thomas Cooper born to a well-to-do family in England.
May 1787– September 1788	Federal Constitution drafted and ratified, new federal government goes into operation, federalists in support and anti-federalists in opposition.
May 4–August 25, 1789	The first federal Congress debates James Madison's proposed amendments to the federal Constitution, finally approving twelve of them. The First Amendment ratified and becomes part of the Constitution on December 15, 1791, along with nine others.
June 17, 1789	French Revolution begins with the creation of the National Assembly. Thomas Jefferson and Thomas Paine support the movement. Initially a constitutional monarchy, the revolution becomes more radical with the creation of a republic, and then a period of repression of all dissent under a Committee of Public Safety. From 1792 through the end of the Napoleonic period in 1815, France periodically found itself at war with its European neighbors, including Great Britain.
1791–1801	First standing national two-party system (Federalists and Republicans) emerges in Congress and then in the electoral districts. Federalists oppose the French Revolution; Republicans support it.
1793–1794	Thomas Cooper emigrates to America with family. Practices law in Western Pennsylvania.

1795–1796	Jay Treaty ratification debates further aggravate divisions between Federalists and Republicans.
1796	John Adams elected president and Thomas Jefferson elected vice president. Federalists control both houses of Congress.
1797	Thomas Cooper petitions President Adams for post as judge in Western Pennsylvania.
February 15, 1798	Republican Congressman Matthew Lyon and Federalist Congressman Roger Griswold do battle in the House chamber.
March 1798	Three emissaries of French foreign minister Talleyrand seek bribes from United States' diplomatic delegation in Paris seeking to negotiate an end to French depredations on American shipping. Called the XYZ Affair, the insult leads Federalists to call for war against France. The war scare ends when President Adams opts for another round of diplomacy in 1800.
June 26, 1798	Benjamin Franklin Bache indicted in federal court for the common law offense of seditious libel.
June–July 1798	Debate and passage, along party lines, of Naturalization Act, Alien Friends Act, Alien Enemies Act, and Sedition Act. Signed by President Adams on July 14, 1798. Sedition Act to expire March 3, 1801.
September 5, 1798	Bache dies of yellow fever, five days before he is to go on trial for violating the federal Sedition Act.
October 6–9, 1798	Matthew Lyon tried and convicted for violating the Sedition Act.
November 16, 1798	Kentucky legislature passes a resolution secretly written by Thomas Jefferson that condemns the Alien and Sedition Acts and calls for state interposition.
December 24, 1798	Virginia House of Delegates passes a resolution secretly written by James Madison condemning the Alien and Sedition Acts but stopping short of state interposition.
November 2, 1799	Thomas Cooper's broadside accuses President Adams of misconduct in office.
January 7, 1800	Madison writes Virginia committee's draft on freedom of expression.
April 12–19, 1800	Indictment and trial of Thomas Cooper for seditious libel. Cooper sentenced to six months in prison.

May 1800– May 1801	Trials of Republican editors and publishers, including William Duane and James Callender, for seditious libel. Twenty-five are arrested, seventeen indictments are filed, eleven tried under the federal act are all convicted. When he becomes president, Jefferson pardons all still in jail.
November 1800– March 1801	Presidential election results in tie between Jefferson and Aaron Burr. House, voting by states, names Jefferson president. In his inaugural, Jefferson asks for party peace and freedom of expression.
1804–1805	Justice Samuel Chase impeached and tried in part for his conduct of the trial of James Callender. He is acquitted by the Senate.
1828	John C. Calhoun secretly writes South Carolina's "Exposition," basing the doctrine of nullification in part on Jefferson's theory of interposition.
1836	"Gag rule" barring reading of abolitionist petitions to Congress defended by Calhoun.
1861–1865	President Abraham Lincoln uses his war powers to suppress pro-Confederate publications during the Civil War.
1917–1918	Espionage Act of 1917 and Sedition Act of 1918 incorporate elements of Sedition Act of 1798, in particular the suppression of speech likely to cause resistance to the war effort.
1919	In *Abrams v. U.S.*, writing in dissent, Justice Oliver Wendell Holmes Jr. introduces the doctrine of a free marketplace of ideas.
1940	Smith Act penalizes words that advocate the violent overthrow of the government.
1957	The U.S. Supreme Court finds that mere advocacy of an ideology calling for the overthrow of the government is not a violation of the Smith Act.
2001	USA Patriot Acts section 805 makes it criminal to give material assistance to terrorists, including published defense of terrorism or terrorist groups, the latter determined by government discretion.

BIBLIOGRAPHICAL ESSAY

Note from the Series Editors: The following bibliographical essay contains the major primary and secondary sources the author consulted for this volume. We have asked all authors in the series to omit formal citations in order to make our volumes more readable, inexpensive, and appealing for students and general readers. In adopting this format, Landmark Law Cases and American Society follows the precedent of a number of highly regarded and widely consulted series.

The foremost source on early history of freedom of the press in America is Leonard Levy, *The Emergence of a Free Press* (New York: Oxford University Press, 1985). The first version of this book was entitled *Legacy of Suppression*, and when it was published, in 1960, it was condemned by liberal jurists, who worried that Levy, a liberal, had betrayed the liberal cause by showing that the origins of the First Amendment were not as robust as they might have been. History and later historians have concluded that Levy was right. Indeed, given the restrictive understanding that the framers had of freedom of speech, the subsequent development of the First Amendment is all the more remarkable.

On the common law of libel, see Zephaniah Swift, *A System of the Laws of the State of Connecticut* . . . (1795), 82; William Blackstone, *Commentaries on the Laws of England* [1769] (London: Routledge, 2001), 4:118; James Wilson to the Pennsylvania Ratification Convention, December 1, 1787, in *Documentary History of the Ratification of the Constitution*, ed. Merrill Jensen et al. (Madison: University of Wisconsin Press, 1976–), 2:455; James Wilson, "Lectures on Law" [1790], in *The Works of James Wilson*, ed. Robert Green McCloskey (Cambridge, Mass.: Harvard University Press, 1967), 2:647; and, generally, Graham Hughes, "Common Law Systems," in *The Fundamentals of American Law*, ed. Alan B. Morrison (New York: Oxford University Press, 1996), 13.

A classic work on the law of libel is Norman L. Rosenberg, *Protecting the Best Men: An Interpretive History of the Law of Libel* (Chapel Hill: University of North Carolina Press, 1986). Rosenberg demonstrates how politics and libel law have from the inception of the nation been uneasy bedfellows. Those in power are always eager to use libel law not only to protect themselves, but to muzzle their critics, as Stanley I. Kutler, *The American Inquisition: Justice and Injustice in the Cold War* (New York: Hill and Wang, 1982), demonstrates. The quote in the text appears on 245.

The source used here for the Zenger trial is Stanley Nider Katz, ed., *A Brief Narrative of the Case and Trial of John Peter Zenger, Printer of the New York Weekly Journal. By James Alexander* (Cambridge, Mass.: Harvard University Press, 1963). Another account of these events is Paul M. Finkelman, ed., *A*

Brief Narrative of the Case and Trial of John Peter Zenger, Printer of the New York Weekly Journal (Union, N.J.: Lawbook Exchange, 2000).

For Madison's address on the Bill of Rights, see Madison, June 8, 1789, in *Register of Debates in Congress [Annals of Congress],* 1st Cong., 1st Sess., 451, 459. On the Bill of Rights debates, see Helen E. Veit, Kenneth R. Bowling, and Charlene Bangs Bickford, eds., *Creating the Bill of Rights: The Documentary Record from the First Federal Congress* (Baltimore: Johns Hopkins University Press, 1991), and Richard Labunski, *James Madison and the Struggle for the Bill of Rights* (New York: Oxford University Press, 2006). A broader documentary survey is Bernard Schwartz, *The Bill of Rights, A Documentary History,* 2 vols. (New York: Chelsea House, 1971). On Madison and the Bill of Rights, see Akhil Reed Amar, *The Bill of Rights: Creation and Reconstruction* (New Haven, Conn.: Yale University Press, 1998), and Jack Rakove, *James Madison and the Creation of the American Republic* (New York: Longman, 2002).

The creation of the two-party system is the subject of Eric L. McKitrick and Stanley M. Elkins's magisterial *The Age of Federalism* (New York: Oxford University Press, 1993). The phrase "damp fireworks" appears on 705. See also James Roger Sharp, *American Politics in the Early Republic: The New Nation in Crisis* (New Haven, Conn.: Yale University Press, 1993), and a now often overlooked gem, Joseph Charles, *The Origins of the American Party System* (Williamsburg, Va.: Colonial Williamsburg, 1956).

The House of Representatives debates on the Sedition Act are on line at the Library of Congress. The *Annals of Congress,* covering the years of the crisis, are part of the American Memory project, "A Century of Lawmaking for a New Nation, U.S. Congressional Documents and Debates, 1774–1875," available at memory.loc.gov/ammem/amlaw/lwac.html. The site warns that "the *Annals* were not published contemporaneously, but were compiled between 1834 and 1856, using the best records available, primarily newspaper accounts. Speeches are paraphrased rather than presented verbatim." All of these collections are searchable by key word.

The texts of the Kentucky and Virginia Resolves can be found at Yale's Avalon site, avalon.law.yale.edu, as well as in the print editions of the papers of Thomas Jefferson and James Madison. Federal court opinions in the free speech cases, including arguments of counsel for cases in the early years, are available from Lexis and Westlaw as well as in Dallas's and Peters's Reports. E.g., for Worrall, see *U.S. v. Worrall,* 2 U.S. (2 Dallas), 384. On the first federal courts, see Maeva Marcus et al., eds., *The Documentary History of the Supreme Court of the United States,* 8 vols. (New York: Columbia University Press, 1985–2007).

The debate over the Sedition Act and the issuance of the Virginia and Kentucky Resolutions, as well as the entire episode, is well covered in James Morton Smith, *Freedom's Fetters: The Alien and Sedition Laws and American Civil Liberties* (Ithaca, N.Y.: Cornell University Press, 1956). A More recent work is

Philip I. Blumberg, *Repressive Jurisprudence in the Early American Republic: The First Amendment and the Legacy of English Law* (New York: Cambridge University Press, 2011), a legal history focusing on the lingering effects of the Sedition Act. Less detailed is John C. Miller, *Crisis in Freedom: The Alien and Sedition Acts* (Boston: Little, Brown, 1951). Smith's book, published at the height of the Cold War, when the United States was fully engaged in the Korean conflict, concluded, "every administration facing a diplomatic crisis such as that which gripped the country in 1798 must weight in the balance the imperative necessity of safeguarding the nation, and the hardly less imperative necessity of permitting men to search freely for the truth. Without freedom of discussion, without the right of examining the methods and objectives of the party in power and criticizing its acts, democracy becomes an empty name" (232–233). On the protests, see Douglas Bradburn, "A Clamor in the Public Mind: Opposition to the Alien and Sedition Acts," *William and Mary Quarterly*, 3rd ser., 65 (July 2008): 365–394, and Kurt T. Lash and Alicia Harrison, "Minority Report: John Marshall and the Defense of the Alien and Sedition Acts," *Ohio State Law Journal* 68 (2007): 450–453. On Jefferson's and Madison's authorship of the resolves, see Adrienne Koch and Henry Ammon, "The Virginia and Kentucky Resolutions: An Episode in Madison's and Jefferson's Defense of Civil Liberties," *William and Mary Quarterly*, 3rd ser., 5 (1948): 145–149, and Kevin R. Gutzman, "A Troublesome Legacy: James Madison and 'The Principles of '98,'" *Journal of the Early Republic* 15 (1995): 569–589.

On Fries's Rebellion, see Paul Douglas Newman, *Fries's Rebellion: The Enduring Struggle for the American Revolution* (Philadelphia: University of Pennsylvania Press, 2004). On street parades and rowdy politics, see David Waldstreicher, *In the Midst of Perpetual Fetes: The Making of American Nationalism, 1776–1820* (Chapel Hill: University of North Carolina Press, 1997).

Primary sources for the indictments under the Sedition Act are the newspapers themselves, available on line in the Evans Collection of early American Imprints, I, and the America's Historical Newspapers, Early American Newspapers, I, both in Archive Americana from Readex. A very readable account of journalism in these years is Eric Burns, *Infamous Scribblers: The Founding Fathers and the Rowdy Beginnings of American Journalism* (New York: PublicAffairs, 2006). See also Richard N. Rosenfeld, *American Aurora: A Democratic Republican Returns* (New York: St. Martins, 1997), and James Tagg, *Benjamin Franklin Bache and the Philadelphia Aurora* (Philadelphia: University of Pennsylvania Press, 1991).

U.S. v. Thomas Cooper, 25 Fed. Cas. 631, no. 14,865 (C.C.D.Pa. 1800), is the formal citation of the prosecution. Thomas Cooper, *An Account of the Trial of Thomas Cooper, of Northumberland, on a Charge of Libel against the President of the United States* (Philadelphia: J. Bioren, 1800), was the contemporary printed version of the trial. The quotations from the trial record all appear in this publication. Another source is John David Lawson, ed., *American State Trials* (Boston, Mass.: Thomas Law Books, 1918), 10:774–812. The National Archives has a website on the trial of Thomas Cooper, at www.archives.gov/education/lessons/sedition-case/. Key documents in facsimile can be found there, as well as the St. George Tucker essay on the sedition law. Forrest K. Lehman, " 'Seditious Libel' on Trial, Political Dissent on the Record: An Account of the Trial of Thomas Cooper As Campaign Literature," *Pennsylvania Magazine of History and Biography* 132 (2008): 117–139, sees the trial as a political occasion manipulated well by Cooper, given that he had no chance to avoid conviction. Adam Smith, *A Theory of Moral Sentiments* (Dublin: Beatty, 1777), 327–328, is the source of the quotation on enlightened self-interest. That no one should be a judge in his own cause is the dictum in Dr. Bonham's Case, 8 Coke's Reports 114 (Court of Common Pleas) (1610). The trial record of James T. Callender was also published, as *The Trial of James Thompson Callender, for Sedition . . .* (Richmond, Va.: Robertson, 1804). On the justices of the U.S. Supreme Court, see Maeva Marcus et al., eds., *The Documentary History of the Supreme Court of the United States, 1789–1800*, vol. 3: *The Justices on Circuit, 1795–1800* (New York: Columbia University Press, 1986), 235–236. (The Ellsworth quotation appears on 235.) The Cooper trial is discussed on 424–434. Reliable and informative throughout, Marcus's work is the first place to look for names and dates of the circuits.

The radical émigrés are tracked in Michael Durey, "Thomas Paine's Apostles: Radical Émigrés and the Triumph of Jeffersonian Republicanism," *William and Mary Quarterly*, 3rd ser., 44 (1987): 662–688. On Cooper, see Dumas Malone, *The Political Life of Thomas Cooper* (New Haven, Conn.: Yale University Press, 1926). Cooper's thoughts on freedom of thought appear in Thomas Cooper, "Philosophical Essays" [1800], in *The Philosophical Writings of Thomas Cooper*, ed. Udo Thiel (London: Continuum, 2001). The quotation from Hugh Henry Brackenridge's *Modern Chivalry* [1815] (Philadelphia: Carey and Hart, 1846), appears on 176–177.

Biographies of the other key figures in the debate reveal motives and ideals. On Jefferson, see Dumas Malone, *Jefferson and His Time*, vol. 4: *Jefferson and the Ordeal of Liberty* (Boston: Little, Brown, 1962); Richard Bernstein, *Thomas Jefferson* (New York: Oxford, 2003); and Joseph J. Ellis, *American Sphinx: The Character of Thomas Jefferson* (New York: Knopf, 1997). A critique of Jefferson's views is Leonard Levy, *Jefferson and Civil Liberties: The Darker Side*, rev. ed. (Chicago: Ivan R. Dee, 1968). On James Madison, see Ralph Ketcham, *James Madison: A Biography* (New York: Macmillan, 1971); Lance Banning, *The Sacred Fire of Liberty: James Madison and the Founding of the Federal Republic* (Ithaca, N.Y.: Cornell University Press, 1995); Drew R. McCoy, *The Last of the Fathers: James Madison and the Republican Legacy* (New York: Cambridge University Press, 1989); and Jack Rakove, *James Madison and the Creation of the*

American Republic, 3rd ed. (New York: Longman, 2006). A defense of Madison's views very different from Rakove and Banning is John Curtis Samples, *James Madison and the Future of Limited Government* (Washington, D.C.: Cato Institute, 2002). For Adams, see Joseph J. Ellis, *Passionate Sage: The Character and Legacy of John Adams* (New York: Norton, 1993), and David McCullough, *John Adams* (New York: Simon and Schuster, 2001). On Gallatin, see Henry Adams's classic *Life of Albert Gallatin* (Philadelphia: Lippincott, 1880). On Otis, another classic is Samuel Eliot Morrison, *Harrison Gray Otis: The Urbane Federalist* (Boston: Houghton, Mifflin, 1969). These are both old-fashioned biographies, as is Malone's, full of authorial judgments and superbly written. On Chase, see Samuel Chase, *Report of the Honorable Samuel Chase . . .* (Baltimore, 1805); Stephen B. Presser and Becky Bair Hurley, "Saving God's Republic: The Jurisprudence of Samuel Chase," *University of Illinois Law Review* 1984 (1984): 771–822; Presser, "In Defense of the Rule of Law and against the Jeffersonians," *Vanderbilt Law Review* 62 (2009): 349–370; and Presser, *The Original Misunderstanding: The English, the Americans and the Dialectic of Federalist Jurisprudence* (Durham, N.C.: Carolina Academic Press, 1991). An older but still useful biography of Chase is Jane S. Elsmere, *Justice Samuel Chase* (Muncie, Ind.: Janvier, 1980). On Chase's impeachment, see Peter Charles Hoffer and N.E.H. Hull, *Impeachment in America, 1635–1805* (New Haven: Yale University Press, 1984). On Timothy Pickering, see Gerald Clarfield, *Timothy Pickering and the American Republic* (Pittsburgh: University of Pittsburgh Press, 1980). An antiquarian reliquary of Pickering letters is Octavius Pickering, *The Life of Timothy Pickering* (Boston: Little, Brown, 1873).

The election of 1800, and the politics preceding it, is the subject of John Ferling, *Adams versus Jefferson: The Tumultuous Election of 1800* (New York: Oxford University Press, 2004); Edward J. Larson, *A Magnificent Catastrophe: The Tumultuous Election of 1800, America's First Presidential Campaign* (New York: Free Press, 2007); and Jay Winik, *The Great Upheaval: America and the Birth of the Modern World, 1788–1800* (New York: Harper, 2007).

On the resolves as precedent for nullification see, e.g., William Freehling, *The Road to Disunion, I: 1776–1854* (New York: Oxford University Press, 1991), 254 and after; Christian G. Fritz, "A Constitutional Middle Ground between Revision and Revolution: A Reevaluation of the Nullification Crisis and the Kentucky and Virginia Resolutions in the Light of Popular Sovereignty," in *Law as Culture, Culture as Law: Essays in Honor of John Philip Reid*, ed. Hendrik Hartog and William E. Nelson (Lanham, Md.: Rowman and Littlefield, 2000), 172–187; Douglas Bradburn, *The Citizenship Revolution: Politics and the Creation of the American Union, 1774–1804* (Charlottesville: University of Virginia Press, 2009), the quote from which appears on 291; Don E. Fehrenbacher, *Constitutions and Constitutionalism in the Slaveholding South* (Athens: University of Georgia Press, 1989); Fehrenbacher, *Sectional Crisis and South-*

ern Constitutionalism (Baton Rouge: Louisiana State University Press, 1995); and John Niven, *John C. Calhoun and the Price of Union* (Baton Rouge: Louisiana State University Press, 1988). The sentiments of southerners on the eve of the Civil War are recounted in Edward Ayers, *In the Presence of Mine Enemies: War in the Heart of America, 1859–1863* (New York: Norton, 2003). On Vallandigham, see Frank L. Klement, *The Limits of Dissent: Clement L. Vallandigham and the Civil War* (New York: Fordham University Press, 1998).

On Debs, see Nick Salvatore, *Eugene V. Debs: Citizen and Socialist*, 2nd ed. (Urbana: University of Illinois Press, 2007). On Holmes and free speech, see *Abrams v. U.S.*, 250 U.S. 616, 629–631 (1919) (Holmes, J.), containing Holmes's famous words. On the Espionage Act of 1917 and Holmes's turnabout, see David Rabban, *Free Speech in Its Forgotten Years* (New York: Cambridge University Press, 1997). For Brandeis's opinion in Whitney, see *Whitney v. California*, 274 U.S. 357, 375 (1926) (Brandeis, J.). On Yates, see *Yates v. U.S.*, 354 U.S. 298, 314, 315 (1957) (Harlan, J.). On *New York Times v. Sullivan*, see Anthony Lewis, *Make No Law: The Sullivan Case and the First Amendment* (New York: Random House, 1991). Brennan's opinion quotation is found in *New York Times v. Sullivan*, 376 U.S. 264, 276, 280 (1964) (Brennan, J.).

There are sweeping accounts of the free speech controversy in America. The first classic work of this genre, Zechariah Chafee, *Freedom of Speech* (New York: Harcourt, 1920), subsequently reissued in updated editions until 1952, was crafted at the height of the first "red scare" after World War I. The battle for First Amendment rights during the second "red scare" in the McCarthy Era occasioned the updating and reissue of the work. More recent works include Akhil Reed Amar, *The Bill of Rights: Creation and Reconstruction* (New Haven, Conn.: Yale University Press, 2000); Michael Kent Curtis, *Free Speech, "The People's Darling Privilege": Struggles for Freedom of Expression in American History* (Durham, N.C.: Duke University Press, 2000); and Geoffrey Stone, *Perilous Times: Free Speech in Wartime from the Sedition Act of 1798 to the War on Terrorism* (New York: Norton, 2004). All three favor a robust reading of the amendment. There are more than 300 general and specific works on the topic today. Even though the subject has broadened to include such collateral issues as academic freedom, hate speech codes, and free speech in advertising, the core remains freedom of speech for those whose words we hate, and who would, if they had the chance, take away our freedom of speech. On this, see Anthony Lewis, *Freedom for the Thought That We Hate: A Biography of the First Amendment* (New York: Basic, 2008) (the quotation in the text appears on 21) and Philippa Strum, *When the Nazis Came to Skokie: Freedom for Speech We Hate* (Lawrence: University Press of Kansas, 2000). As Lewis wrote in his *Freedom for the Thought That We Hate*, 1, "the American commitment to freedom of speech and press is the more remarkable because it emerged from legal and political origins that were highly repressive."

INDEX

Abolitionists, 122
Abrams v. U.S., 125–127
Adams, John, 2, 31
  and Alien and Sedition Acts,
    viii–ix
  and Bache, 4
  on Chase, 81
  and Cooper pardon, 110
  and Cooper trial, 85, 89–90,
    90–91, 96
  and France, 113
  and Robbins case, 75
  Thoughts on Government of, 67, 80
Adams, John Quincy, and "gag
  rule," 122
Alexander, James, 10, 11
Alien and Sedition Acts, 8, 48, 116
Alien Enemies Act of 1798, 32–33
Alien Friends Act of 1798, 33, 100
Alien Registration Act of 1940
  (Smith Act), 127
Amar, Akhil Reed, 118
American Revolution, ix–x, 2
  and free press, 17, 18, 39
Anti-federalists, 78

Bache, Benjamin Franklin, 1–5, 7–8
Bill of Rights, viii–ix, 21–24
Blackstone, William, 9, 19, 41, 117
Brackenridge, Hugh Henry, 75–76
Bradburn, Douglas, 56
Brandeis, Louis, 130
Brennan, William, 130
Burk, John Daly, 7
Burke, Edmund, 29
Burr, Aaron, 90

Calhoun, John C., x, 120
  Exposition of, 120–122

and nullification, 120
and slavery, 123
Callender, James, 2–3, 7
  trial of, 86–87, 114–115
Character witnesses, 106–107
Chase, Samuel, ix, 80–81
  at Callender trial, 114–115
  and common law, 6
  at Cooper Trial, 85–110
  impeached, 119
  and *U.S. v. Cooper*, 83–84
  and *Worrall*, 6–7
Civic virtue ideology, 39
Civil War, 124
Clinton v. Jones (1997), 90
Cobbett, William, 4
Coke, Edward, 104
Common law
  in colonies, 12
  federal reception of, 6, 7, 37–39,
    45, 119
Compact theory, of Constitution,
  55, 61, 121
"Concurrent majority," doctrine of,
  121
Congress (U.S.), and Bill of Rights,
  23–24
Contempt of assembly, 17
Contempt of court, 13, 83
Cooper, Thomas, ix, 8, 111–112
  in England, 28–30
  indicted, 83–84, 85
  literary technique of, 75
  in New York, 28
  Political Essays of, 77–79, 111
  and *To the Printer*, 74–75
  and trial record, 82–83
  tried, 85–110
Cosby, William, 10, 11, 14

Courts
  in England, 16
  in U.S., 80
Croswell, Harry, 57
Cushing, William, 116

Dallas, Alexander James
  and Bache, 6–7
  at Cooper Trial, 87, 94
  at trial of Duane, 115
  and *Worrall*, 6–7
Debs, Eugene V., 125
DeLancey, James, 10, 13, 14, 16
Delegated powers, in Constitution, 61
Democracy, 64–65, 77–78, 104
Dr. Bonham's Case, 103–104
Duane, William, 2, 7
  trial of, 115

Election of 1796, 30, 31
Election of 1800, x, 47, 52, 62, 73, 101, 108, 109
Elkins, Stanley, 115
Ellsworth, Oliver, 116
Espionage Act of 1917, 124–125
Establishment Clause, 24
"Exposition and Protest," x

"Farewell Address," of Washington, 30
Federalism, 56
Federalist, 21, 64
Federalist Party, vii, 79
  and England, viii, 40
  and France, 4, 27
  and Hamilton, 25
  and Sedition Act, 34–37, 43, 47, 50, 72, 73, 116
Federalists, and the Constitution, 21
Fenno, John, 3, 4
  and Cooper trial, 92, 105, 106

First Amendment, 15, 24, 39, 56, 128
Fourteenth Amendment, 22
Fox's Libel Act of 1792, 17
France
  diplomacy of, viii
  near war with, 3, 27, 32–33, 113
Franklin, Benjamin, 19–20
Freedom of the Press
  in colonies, 10, 15–19
  in England, 9, 23
  in Pennsylvania, 18, 41–42, 43
  and political opinion, 30, 82–83
  in Virginia, 24, 42, 56
French Directory, 3
French Revolution, vii–viii, 3, 26, 29
Fries's Rebellion, 82

"Gag rule," 122
  and dangerous tendency test, 122
Gallatin, Albert, 36
  and Cooper trial, 98, 99
  on Sedition Act, 42, 44–47
Gerry, Elbridge, 58–59
"Glorious Revolution" (England), 22
Grand juries, 83
Griswold, Roger, 31–32

Hamilton, Alexander, 2, 24–25
  domestic program of, 25
  and election of 1800, 113
  and Federalist Party, vii
  on Sedition Act, 34
Hamilton, Andrew, 10, 11. *See also* Zenger, John Peter: case of
Harper, Robert Goodloe, 98, 99
Hartford Convention, 58
Holmes, Oliver Wendell, Jr., 125–127

Impeachment, 119
Impressment, viii
Ingersoll, Jared, 115

Interposition, doctrine of, 61–62, 119
Irony, in history, 113
Israel, Israel, 84

Jarndyce v. Jarndyce, 97
Jay Treaty, 3, 28, 32, 40
Jefferson, Thomas, ix, 2, 53–54
  and Burr trial, 90
  on federal government, 59
  on First Amendment, 59
  and Kentucky Resolves, 54–58
  and libels, 118
  as president, 117–118, 119
Jewish community (of Philadelphia), 84
Judiciary Act of 1789, 38, 87
Judiciary Act of 1801, 118–119
Juries, 13–14, 16, 102, 103, 104, 107, 109

Kagan, Elena, vii
Kentucky Resolves, x, 54–58, 120
Kutler, Stanley, 128

Law and society, 130
Law of evidence, 93–95, 98, 99, 105
Lawyering, 38–39, 41, 75–76, 102
Levy, Leonard, 71
Lewis, Anthony, 128
Libel, civil, 5, 15, 132
Libel, criminal, 5
Lincoln, Abraham, and freedom of the press, 123–124
Livingston, Edward, 35
  and Cooper trial, 98
Lloyd, James, 34
Logan, George, 32
"Loose construction," doctrine of, 45, 57
Loyalists, 17–18

Lyon, Matthew, 31–32
  and Cooper trial, 97, 98
  trial of, 72

Madison, James, ix, 20, 21
  and Bill of Rights, 21–24, 69–70
  on checks and balances, 67–68
  on federal government, 61
  and First Amendment, 20
  on First Amendment, 62, 66–67
  on Hamilton, 64
  and report on freedom of expression, 64–71
  and Virginia Resolves, 60–64
Magna Carta, 23
Malone, Dumas, 111
Marshall, John, 90
"Massive resistance," 128
McKitrick, Eric, 115
Milton, John, 9
Morris, Lewis, 11

Naturalization Act of 1798, 32, 57
Necessary and Proper Clause, 37, 44, 45, 65, 66
Nelson, Thomas, 114
Neutrality, 28
New York Times v. Sullivan, 131
Ninth Amendment, 22
No prior restraint, doctrine of, 9, 40, 46, 52–53, 71
Nullification, doctrine of, 56, 57–58, 62, 71, 119–120

Original intent, 66
Otis, Harrison Gray, 36
  and Sedition Act, 35, 37–43

Paine, Thomas, 30
Parliament, 12
Paterson, William, 116
Patriot Acts, vii

Peters, Richard, 81
    at Cooper Trial, 87, 93, 99, 105
    and *Worrall*, 6–7
Philadelphia, 1
Philadelphia Aurora, 2
Pickering, John, 119
Pickering, Timothy, 73–74
    and Cooper, 74–75, 80
    at Cooper trial, 85, 96
Political Parties, ideology of, 26
Presser, Stephen, 7
Priestly, Joseph, 30
Process Act of 1789, 38

Rawle, William, ix
    and Bache, 4, 5
    closing statement of at Cooper
        trial, 107–109
    and Cooper, 80
    at Cooper trial, 84, 86, 92, 93,
        100, 105
"Reign of terror," 26, 27
Republican Party, vii, 78
    and England, viii
    and France, 28
    and Jefferson, 25
    and Madison, 25
    response to Sedition Act, 50,
        51–52, 53, 115
"republican virtue," 2
Robbins, Jonathan, case of, 75

Sedition Act (of 1798), ix, vii, 33–48,
    132
    procedures in, 47–48, 51
    text of, 48–49
    trials under, 113–115
Sedition Act (of 1918), 124–125
Seditious libel
    chilling effect of, 43, 52, 62
    and dangerous tendency test, 19,
        108

defined, 5
    in England, 9, 12, 82
    and federal law, 6, 19, 37–47
    and political opinion, 20, 43, 47,
        109–110
    and truth, 13
Segregation, 129
Sherman, Roger, 24
"Show trial," 82
Slander, 5
Slavery, 123
Slave trade, 57
Smith, Adam, 103
States' rights, doctrine of, 55
"Strict construction," doctrine of,
    44, 46
*Sunbury and Northumberland
    Gazette*, 75
Supremacy Clause, 55
Swift, Zephaniah, 18–19

Taylor, George, 62–63
Tenth Amendment, 46
Treaty of 1778, 27
Tucker, St. George, 116–117

U.S. Supreme Court, and Cooper
    trial, 116
U.S. v. Nixon (1974), 90

Vallandigham, Clement, case of,
    124–125
Van Damm, Rip, 10
Virginia Resolves, x, 60–64
"Virginia rule," 86, 114

Washington, George, 2, 65
Whiskey Rebellion, 81–82, 84, 101
Whitney v. California, 130
Wilson, James, 19
World War I, 125
World War II, 127

Worrall v. U.S., 6–7, 38
Wythe, George, 53

"XYZ Affair," 32

Yates v. U.S., 127–128

Zenger, John Peter, x
  case of, 10–17